Living with the Enemy

Coping with the stress of chronic illness using CBT, mindfulness and acceptance

Ray Owen

Routledge
Taylor & Francis Group

LONDON AND NEW YORK

First published 2014
by Routledge
2 Park Square, Milton Park, Abingdon, Oxon OX14 4RN

and by Routledge
711 Third Avenue, New York, NY 10017

Routledge is an imprint of the Taylor & Francis Group, an informa business

British Library Cataloguing in Publication Data
A catalogue record for this book is available from the British Library

Library of Congress Cataloging in Publication Data
Owen, Ray, 1964-
Living with the enemy : coping with the stress of chronic illness using cbt, mindfulness and acceptance / Ray Owen. -- First Edition.
pages cm
Includes bibliographical references.
1. Stress (Psychology) 2. Cognitive therapy. 3. Mindfulness-based cognitive therapy. I. Title.
BF575.S75O94 2013
155.9'16--dc23
2013005513

ISBN: 978-0-415-52119-2 (hbk)
ISBN: 978-0-415-52120-8 (pbk)
ISBN: 978-0-203-79797-6 (ebk)

Typeset in New Century Schoolbook and Frutiger
by Saxon Graphics Ltd, Derby

MIX
Paper from
responsible sources
FSC
www.fsc.org   **FSC® C013604**   Printed and bound by CPI Group (UK) Ltd, Croydon, CR0 4YY

Dedication

To all the people who have encouraged and supported me over the years.

To my family, who do that more than anyone.

And to the memory of my parents, who did that first.

Contents

List of figures

List of exercises

Preface

'This isn't living, it's just existing!'

It doesn't matter how many times people have said that to me, it's always sad to hear.

On this occasion, I was with Mandy, a married woman in her mid-40s who had been referred to me by her specialist nurse. About ten years ago, when both her children were toddlers, she'd been diagnosed with rheumatoid arthritis, a serious condition that causes inflammation of the joints, pain, stiffness and fatigue.

There followed years of investigation and different drug treatments. Despite frequent and severe 'flare-ups' of the condition, she'd apparently remained upbeat and positive throughout this time, and impressed her care team by how well she handled the disease and its treatment alongside raising a family and carrying on with her career.

For the last year or so, she had been physically a little more stable; even though the long-term damage to wrist and finger joints hadn't improved, she had had fewer new attacks, less pain and a bit more energy.

Yet it was now that her mood had taken a tumble – her nurse described her as tearful and withdrawn for the first time since knowing her. And when I met Mandy, she agreed that she felt wretched.

It wasn't so bad while I was tied up in all the treatment and having the bad attacks. Even the worst flare-ups felt like something I was willing to fight my way through in order to be around for my kids. But since it's stabilised a bit, I keep wondering ... is this it? Is this all there is for me?

Sure I can get through the day and do most of the things the kids need me to. But the cost of keeping fighting like this is so wearying, and getting through the day is all I really manage; my job went when the company was taken over, and who'd want someone with my sickness record? Luckily, John earns just about enough to keep us, but I was going to have a career too; that's gone now.

I like being a mother, but I can't do all the proper mum things like play games with the kids or take them camping – it causes pain, and anyway I've not got the flexibility or the manual dexterity. Even though most days aren't too bad now, I can't actually *rely* on being well on a particular day – so it's hard to plan days out, or be sure that I can be at their Christmas concert or something.

I've been getting so frustrated about it that I'm snapping at the kids – and at John. Our relationship's changed in the last couple of years; I can't stand seeing what my body looks like now in a mirror, and I can't bear the thought of him touching me like this, so the physical side of our marriage has gone.

I spend half the time thinking about how much better life used to be, and half worrying about when the next attack comes. I tell myself that maybe one day there'll be a cure, or I'll at least have no symptoms at all, and then I can get on with the life I should have been having. But that doesn't seem to be happening.

So every day's a battle against my arthritis – and it's like the war's using up all my energy and my will to carry on, but I'm just not winning. Like I said, it's only existing; it's not living.

Who could argue with any of that? A strong, determined and resourceful woman who'd kept going despite intense physical suffering, real limitations and major treatments. And now she was stuck.

I told her that, and then carried on:

The thing is, Mandy, you're telling *me* that you're not winning this war, even with all that resilience and commitment to keep going for your family's sake. Maybe it's time to try a different approach, to stop using yourself up in this war against your arthritis that isn't getting you anywhere. Maybe if you can learn a way to live with that enemy, rather than use all your energy fighting it, you'll be less stuck. And then you've got a chance to start really living again, rather than just existing. How about we give it a go?

And in simply beginning to talk about the situation that way, we'd already taken the first step ...

Acknowledgements

The contents of this book come from two main sources: the innovative thinking, research and development of leading therapists and researchers, and my own experience of using those techniques with a range of people living with long-term physical health problems.

I would therefore like to thank those therapists and researchers responsible for developing the approach used in this book – Acceptance and Commitment Therapy (ACT) – including Professor Steve Hayes, Kirk Strosahl and Kelly Wilson, and more recently Dr Russ Harris, along with the whole ACT community who contribute to its continued evolution via the Association of Contextual Behavioural Science web forum.

I would also like to thank all the clients with long-term conditions I have seen, and their families. None of them appears directly in this book; all case studies are fictional, but they are informed by the experiences of people I have met.

Finally, I would like to thank colleagues – especially Kate Jones for detailed reviewing of drafts – friends and my family who have supported me in writing this book. Particular thanks go to my wife, Ronya, both for general moral support and for tireless reviewing and proofreading, and to the very supportive team at Routledge.

Despite all their help and attention to detail, however, any remaining omissions or inaccuracies are my own responsibility.

Knowing the enemy

1.1 The scale of the problem

In Western countries, up to a third of us have a long-term physical health condition: something like diabetes, arthritis, asthma or any of a range of chronic illnesses that affect daily life.[1] By the time we reach 60, that has risen to more than half of us, and more still if we count high blood pressure. And many of us will have more than one of them.

This is a huge problem, in lots of ways.

For society as a whole, that means a large portion of the workforce is either less able to work productively or completely unable to. It's also a lot of skills and effort being lost to services and industry, and a huge amount of financial support required to meet even the basic needs of those who can't work any longer. Not to mention huge costs for the healthcare system; up to 70 per cent of the UK's NHS spending is on long-term conditions (LTCs).[2]

More importantly for the individual, that's a lot of physical suffering. Depending on which LTC we're talking about, it could be pain, fatigue, breathing difficulties, problems moving or balancing, losing consciousness, restrictions on eating, loss of vision, insomnia or any of dozens of other specific symptoms.

With the physical symptoms may come restrictions on the ability to work, to care for family members or for yourself, or to pursue pleasures either because you're physically unable to or you can't afford the cost anymore.

And there's another area of life where LTCs can have a huge effect: the impact on emotions, on thoughts and actions.

In everyday speech, we might talk about these as the 'stress' of illness, or more precisely the psychological effects. And these can be just as damaging to a person's quality of life as the physical or practical effects of the illness.

On the surface, Bill's doing well in life. At 43, he has a wife and two daughters whom he loves, he has a responsible job in management that he enjoys, and while he's far from rich, the family is financially stable.

Ten years ago, Bill was diagnosed with multiple sclerosis (MS). He'd had one previous episode of pain behind the eyes and blurring of vision, but that had cleared up by itself. When it came back, this time accompanied by dizziness and weakness, his doctors put him through a series of investigations, and finally diagnosed MS. With treatment, that attack passed, though he's been left with some permanent effects. He can have days when his balance isn't great, and he has quite a lot of stiffness in his muscles – particularly his legs. He's normally OK around the office or home, but has to use a walking stick if he's going any distance outside. He also runs out of energy more quickly than he used to, especially on hot days. There was a 'flare-up' of his condition a couple of years ago, where all his symptoms got worse and the eyesight problems came back, but again drug treatment brought that to an end fairly quickly, and he was soon back to the same long-term symptoms as before, though maybe a little bit worse.

Everyone around Bill tells him he copes brilliantly; the restrictions don't stop him from being an effective employee and a good husband and father.

Yet others don't see him at 2.00 a.m., wide awake, worrying about the future – what if he has another flare-up, and the symptoms get even worse? What if he ends up in a wheelchair? Becomes incontinent or impotent? What if he becomes a burden to his wife and family? What if he loses his job and the family have no income? Bill's nights are full of these worries, and it's only by keeping busy all day long that he quietens them.

What we see in Bill's story is someone who has adjusted practically to his LTC, but for whom the psychological effect (worry in his case) is bringing more misery than the symptoms themselves.

And that's what this book is about: why we get stressed in this way, and what to do about it.

Unfortunately, the answer is not to get rid of the LTC or its symptoms because, by their very nature, the conditions cannot be cured by any surgery or drug that has been invented so far (if they could, they wouldn't be LTCs). And, equally, most of them will produce symptoms that cannot be managed simply and without side-effects; again, if they could, then these conditions wouldn't create problems of the scale discussed above.

So the challenge will be to find a way to live life as best we can even with those conditions and their symptoms as part of our lives.

1.2 The nature of long-term conditions

It's worth being clear about what I mean by LTCs – or, to be even more precise, long-term physical health conditions. The World Health Organization defined LTCs as those requiring 'ongoing management over a period of years or decades'.[3] Other definitions emphasise that these are conditions that cannot (at present) be cured. They could be ones that may directly or indirectly be fatal at some point, but the term isn't usually used for diseases that have a very short life-expectancy right from the point they first appear.

Many people are probably more familiar with the term 'chronic illness' (hence my using it in the subtitle of this book), and we are talking about pretty much the same thing. However, some LTCs – for example, long-term pain after losing a limb – can't really be called illnesses or diseases; that's why healthcare services now far more commonly talk about LTCs than 'chronic illness'.

You may also notice I mentioned earlier that I would be talking more specifically about long-term *physical* health conditions. It is certainly true that there are long-term mental health conditions such as bipolar disorder, psychotic conditions (e.g. schizophrenia), severe long-term depression or life-long obsessive-compulsive problems. Sadly, in some cases these cannot be cured, nor do they always disappear by themselves. And these problems can be just as devastating as a physical health problem.

Now, many of these types of problem have been shown to benefit to some degree at least from the techniques I'll be discussing in this book. However, I'm not going to focus on them, partly because it's much harder to say when we're genuinely 'stuck with' components of these (e.g. mood swings, panic attacks); whether through treatment or by spontaneous improvement, such problems sometimes recede in a way that we're unlikely to see in conditions like MS. And that's different to dealing with MS like Bill's, or many of the other long-term physical health problems that people can suffer, where the underlying causes of the problem are not going to go away.

The second reason for not focusing on long-term mental health problems is this: one of the reasons they can be so debilitating is that the very processes we're going to be using to cope better (thinking, choosing what to pay attention to, planning ahead) are the very things that are most affected by those mental health conditions. Again, I'd want to point out that these same techniques can still be used for people with those problems – it's just that in some cases we need to go about it in a slightly different way. And that's also why we'll be excluding LTCs like dementia or significant brain injury.

Which isn't to say that our purely 'physical' LTCs don't bring major psychological problems along with them.

Desmond doesn't feel like the man he used to be. For someone who worked in heavy industry, enjoyed gardening and socialising, aging was bound to be a difficult thing to adjust to.

But in the last few years, everything seems to have gone wrong for him. Not only did he lose his wife to cancer five years ago, but his health has deteriorated sharply. He has a serious lung disease – chronic obstructive pulmonary disease or COPD – which means he gets breathless very easily doing even the simplest tasks, or walking the shortest distances. That's put an end to his gardening, to standing pitchside watching football in the park, and even walking to the social club. On top of this, he has diabetes, no doubt made worse by the amount of weight he has put on since becoming less active. He's been told that he risks all sorts of complications, including blindness and possibly ending up having a limb amputated, if he doesn't take better care of his diet. But somehow he just can't be bothered. Mostly, he just stays in his flat, half-watching TV, eating and drinking the wrong things and feeling like life's just miserable.

Sadly, Desmond's not alone; one study found that half of people with COPD had clinically significant levels of anxiety or depression.[4] And part of the reason, especially in Desmond's case, is not so much the physical symptoms themselves (difficult though they may be), but what they take away from the person's life. He'd already lost his working life, then his wife, but then the illnesses took away his ability to enjoy gardening, watching sport, going out for a drink, and (if were to follow dietary advice) his favourite foods and beer too. Because, like many older people, Desmond has more than one LTC, the effects of one can complicate dealing with the other; because his COPD leaves him less able to get out and be active, he stays still and comfort eats, worsening his diabetes. It's not surprising that he's unhappy with his life at the moment.

But how can things get better?

For Desmond, things getting better can't mean the COPD or diabetes vanishing (because they won't), and unfortunately, even with the best support and rehab, he's unlikely to be able to dig his allotment or stand on a freezing touchline on a December Sunday morning. And a diet of lager and microwave curry isn't suddenly going to become health food for him.

In his case, the challenge is going to be finding a life worth living that doesn't involve the things that his illnesses have taken away from him permanently. I'll be talking at length about that before the end of this book.

So we see from Desmond's experience that the physical aspects of LTCs are interwoven with the psychological.

Both these aspects of health are also intimately connected to the setting they take place in, whether that's a physical setting (e.g. living in a cold, damp place), a practical one (e.g. not having enough money to heat your home properly) or a social one (e.g. being isolated and having no one to help out when you're ill). For many people, it may be the case that any one of the problems they face might be manageable, but it's the combination of physical and psychological problems and their situation that causes the difficulty.

Caroline finds it hard to get past the thought that 'It wasn't meant to be like this'. At 61 years old, with husband Geoff four years her senior, this was when they'd planned to be enjoying a carefree retirement – she from part-time teaching, he from his accountancy job at a large corporation. But events haven't worked out that way.

Much of her spare time has been dedicated to her family – especially caring for her frail elderly mother and providing childcare to allow her grown-up daughters to work.

Then 18 months ago, Geoff was involved in a bad car accident and sustained a serious head injury. It wasn't clear he'd survive, so everyone is pleased that his physical recovery has been as strong as it has. Unfortunately, other areas of recovery haven't been so complete – his concentration and memory remain very poor, he cannot plan or organise himself at all, and he has become much more short-tempered, and is sometimes rude and aggressive to those around him, especially Caroline. Now she finds she is having to take responsibility for all areas of their lives and care for Geoff, as well as support her mother and her daughters.

No wonder, then, that her irritable bowel syndrome (IBS) is getting worse; when under stress, she has bad stomach pain, her appetite goes and she often has to dash

> to the toilet; all of which makes it even harder to keep up
> with her responsibilities.
>   It really wasn't meant to be like this.

So for Caroline, just like Desmond and Bill whom we've already met, the LTC has physical problems; it has an impact on her ability to function within the world she lives in and causes significant psychological suffering, which itself makes the other problems worse.

1.3 The approach we'll take in this book

Given that our lives are affected by health problems in all these different ways, and how closely they are connected, it may seem odd that this book focuses almost totally on coping with the *psychological* aspects of these LTCs.

There are, however, several reasons why this makes sense.

- *The physical effects of different LTCs vary.*
  Some symptoms may occur in several different conditions (fatigue, pain), but others are far more specific: loss of consciousness may be part of one person's epilepsy, but it is unlikely to be a symptom of Caroline's IBS. And the causes, of course, also vary hugely.
- *Symptom management approaches vary.*
  If you have one of these conditions, you are probably already aware of the vast amount of information on the possible benefits of different drugs, diet, exercise regimes and even self-management techniques; if you're feeling pain, do you sit down, lie down for a sleep, reduce activity but still keep going, stop and do stretching exercises, take medication? The answer may be different if the pain is part of a years-old chronic pain problem as opposed to an acute flare-up of eye-nerve pain in MS.

No one book could address the range of physical symptoms and offer effective and safe advice on symptom management across all of the possible conditions (and, indeed, combinations of conditions).

Yet there are some things that are far more shared between different conditions and living situations. Irrespective of the particular diagnosis, we may suffer from anxiety, or anger, sadness, shame or guilt. We may worry to the point of distraction during the day and lie awake at night. Our thoughts can become scattered, preventing us from concentrating, remembering or achieving. We can become so stressed that we can't face simple prospects like shopping for food. Or so sad that we withdraw from friends, family and the very activities that normally bring us pleasure. We can lose our sense of purpose so profoundly that life feels as if it is only about coping with the illness, or – worse still – that it has no point at all. It can lead us to contemplate suicide, and it leads some to act on those thoughts.

And these things, which are in their own ways every bit as disabling as physical symptoms, aren't confined to any one condition, type of person or social setting. These psychological pressures may come from more than one condition, or the interaction of that condition with other aspects of life.

They deserve our close attention; they will require detailed exploration and a serious effort at applying new ways of dealing with them.

That's why, I believe, managing these common but difficult effects of LTCs deserves a book of its own: because doing them justice can't be just one chapter in a book full of advice on diet, exercise and medication of a particular illness.

And, although they're not the main focus of this book, most of the same principles and ideas can be applied to disabilities such as impairments of movement or senses that arise by illness, accident or development from birth onwards.

That brings us to one of the central messages of this book. Some of the symptoms and limitations brought by LTCs may be unavoidable. And experiencing troubling thoughts and strong emotions may be too – but you can learn to handle those thoughts and feelings differently so that they don't take over your life so much.

Alina loved her first few years in the UK. From age 18 she and a group of friends travelled across from Poland each summer to do seasonal agricultural work. Though it was physically very demanding, had long hours and her living conditions were very basic, she had fun. And with good reason: she was with friends, they had few responsibilities, she was attractive and popular, and enjoyed feeling fit from the hours in the fields, and even went running on her day off.

And when she settled more permanently, things were still good, though she was glad to start working in the hotel industry as she was beginning to find the fruit-picking caused her aches and pains. Unfortunately, the pain carried on even when she switched jobs and now affects many parts of her body. She's good at her job, having quickly risen to duty manager at the hotel, and can manage her pain well enough so long as she can have the occasional sit down. That comes at a price, though; she has very little energy left at the end of the day, is in stronger pain by the evening, and her sleep is disturbed. Her GP has told her it's a condition called fibromyalgia, but there doesn't seem to be a cure.

She's also stopped socialising – she always feels too tired for it and ends up sitting at home instead. Because she doesn't exercise either, she's started to put on some weight, making her feel less attractive, less positive about herself and (she suspects) increasing the pain in her back and legs.

Worse still, she actually finds herself feeling nervous in social situations, or even crowded places. Her mind goes into overdrive: 'What if the pain gets too much, and there's nowhere to sit?', 'People who know me are thinking "she's so fat now"', 'Other people are in couples – no one will ever find me attractive again', 'Life used to be so much better than this'.

All in all, maybe it's easier just to get through work as best she can each day, then stay at home.

For Alina, the chronic pain problem is (just about) manageable. What's limiting her life more is the way her mind reacts to it: the upsetting thoughts and feelings, and how they have led her to give up on everything in life other than work.

Note the fact that, just because her own mind is her biggest hurdle, it doesn't mean that the pain is insignificant, nor is it imaginary. And the same will be true throughout this book. It's such a fundamental element of this approach that it's worth spelling it out as clearly as possible:

> These long-term conditions are real; they are not imaginary or exaggerated. Improving our quality of life with a condition by approaching it differently does *not* mean it was 'all in the mind'.

I write this as a psychologist working in the field of physical, not mental, health. The clients I see, and have been seeing for the last 20 years, are people with cancer, lung diseases, MS, epilepsy, motor neurone disease, brain injury and genetic conditions. When they use the principles I'll discuss in this book, and their lives improve, it isn't because those conditions have somehow been cured – that's relatively uncommon in the people I see. It's because they've found a different way of moving forward with that condition, by learning a different approach to their troubling thoughts, unwanted emotions, distressing symptoms and restricted choices: a different approach to their suffering.

It's because the problems are real, and the suffering is real, that I've called this book *Living with the Enemy*; the LTC is (almost) entirely a force for bad in the sufferer's life. It's hard *not* to see it as an enemy. It would, of course, be everyone's first choice to get rid of this enemy, but that's not possible at this moment (if it was, it wouldn't be an LTC). What's more, we cannot afford to keep trying to achieve that impossible goal, as constantly being at war with it will not only fail but will further get in the way of living our life.

Neither is the message that, in some way, we can regard that condition as a friend, and take away its impact by thinking positive thoughts about it.

And it doesn't mean that we surrender, give up and allow it to run our lives completely.

The key message of this book is that, when dealing with the stress of LTCs, the answer is not to struggle harder against that enemy, nor to submit to it, but rather to find a way of 'living with the enemy', freeing you to get on with living a life that you value.

1.4 The approach: ACT

The approach I'll be discussing here is one form of Cognitive Behavioural Therapy (CBT). At the moment, CBT is one of the most widely used forms of psychological therapy, which has demonstrated a great deal of success in a wide variety of problems from panic attacks to psychotic problems in the mental health arena,[5] and across a range of physical health conditions including chronic pain,[6] tinnitus[7] and breathing difficulties[8] amongst others.

To be precise, CBT isn't actually one form of therapy but rather a general classification of certain types of therapy that differ in small ways and large and that offer a bewildering range of abbreviations and acronyms, including REBT (Rational Emotive Behaviour Therapy),[9] DBT (Dialectical Behaviour Therapy)[10] and CT (Cognitive Therapy).[11]

For the most part, the form of CBT we'll be applying here is called Acceptance and Commitment Therapy,[12] and is itself shortened to ACT. We always pronounce it like the word 'act', not 'Ay See Tee', because, as I hope will become clear, it is ultimately about taking action to make our lives better. It's one of the approaches sometimes called 'third wave CBT', and although it's a fairly recent approach, it is already recognised as an 'Evidence-Based Practice',[13] having an impressive amount of evidence for helping people cope and live better with a range of difficulties in life.

To take just one example, some of the skills I'm going to teach you were added into an existing one-day education programme for people with diabetes. Not only did the participants report that they were managing their diabetes better three months later, but their blood-sugar levels were measurably healthier than the group who just had the normal education programme.[14]

I'll take you through the main components of ACT as they apply to living better with a chronic health condition. Much of what I say is based on groups I've been running for the last few years to teach these skills to people with health problems. And while a book doesn't give you the companionship of going through the programme with others in a similar position, on the other hand it should give us room to go into the details in much more depth than my seven two-hour classes.

A word, though, about what I won't be giving. Because (as described above) the physical aspects of LTCs vary so much more than the psychological, I won't be discussing the physical management of symptoms or disease-specific coping strategies. So this book isn't the place to look for dietary advice, exercise regimes, guides to drugs or complementary medicines. And, even though topics like fatigue and pain will come up time and again, this isn't about either pain-management or fatigue-management as such, as both have many aspects that may differ according to whether your fatigue arises from – say – chemotherapy side-effects or chronic fatigue syndrome/ME.

My advice would always be to find out the details of your specific LTC from people you trust – your GP and healthcare team, reputable information providers and patient associations. And if you read anything in this book that you think might be inappropriate to your specific condition, then check it out with one of them. As I've said above, I've used these techniques with people with a very wide range of problems, but sadly I don't know *you* personally, and so ultimately it'll have to be your decision (with advice, I hope) whether you need to adapt or even ignore anything I say.

As we go through the book, you'll find suggested activities to try. I know when I read a book like this, I notice an urge to skip forward and tell myself I'll come back to the exercise later – and sometimes don't. I'd encourage you to give the exercises a proper attempt when you get to them, because experience of doing something often teaches us more than just reading about it. The time and effort of doing the suggested activities should be a price worth paying.

In order to see how the ideas we'll be learning about can apply in practice in the lives of people with LTCs, we'll follow the examples of the people I've already introduced – Desmond, Caroline, Bill and Alina. Because it wouldn't be fair of me to describe in this book real individuals I've worked with, I've invented each of them. However, their experiences and problems are based very much on those I've encountered time and again in my work. I wouldn't be at all surprised for any one of them to walk through my office door next week.

So let's proceed and look in more detail at the struggles they're facing.

Key points

- Chronic illnesses (long-term physical health conditions) are very common, and can have major psychological effects as well as physical and practical ones.
- How you handle specific physical symptoms may vary between LTCs, but how you handle the psychological effects has more in common between them.
- Coping can't depend on curing the LTC or making all its symptoms go away (as neither is currently possible); instead it involves learning to live differently with what's happening.
- The aim is to avoid either being in a constant fight with your LTC or giving up, but rather 'living with the enemy'.
- This book will explore a way of doing that based on a form of CBT that emphasises acceptance and mindfulness, called Acceptance and Commitment Therapy, or ACT.
- Because I can't know your personal circumstances, if anything this book recommends seems incompatible with your condition, you should check that out with your healthcare team before deciding whether to do it.
- At times I'll suggest exercises (psychological ones rather than physical exercise); you will probably gain more from the book if you do them as you go along.

Getting stuck in the struggle

2.1 Untangling the mess

Today has been a bad day for Caroline.

She promised to look after her youngest grandson so that her daughter could attend a training day at work. But she forgot that her husband Geoff had a physiotherapy appointment, and trying to get him organised and out of the door for that is half a day's work in itself. Now she's running late for the appointment, snapping both at Geoff and her grandson Alfie for causing delays, and she can't even find a parking space at the hospital.

As she drives in circles, the tension in her shoulders starts a headache … and sure enough, her gut is beginning to play up; she's suffering bouts of griping pain in her bowels, and beginning to panic more about finding a toilet in time than about being late for Geoff's appointment.

'I can't cope with all this,' she thinks for the thousandth time, and feels more overwhelmed still.

I suspect many of us have had a day like Caroline's and can sympathise with that overwhelmed feeling – as if one huge mess of demands, bad feelings, stressed thoughts, physical symptoms and rushing around has taken over.

And if you have an LTC, then there are more sources of pressure and a bigger range of consequences of that pressure.

If we're to learn how to deal differently with these situations, we're going to have to start making some sense of that mess. And that's where some of the ideas from CBT can help.

Looking at Caroline's story again, rather than finding it a mess of experiences we can begin to pick out some different elements. Here's how we would traditionally divide them up in CBT:

> *Trigger (or 'Context')*: trying to get things done for other people.
>
> *Thoughts*: 'I can't find a parking space', 'We'll be late', 'I need the toilet', 'I can't cope'.
>
> *Feelings (or 'Emotions')*: annoyed, guilty, anxious, overwhelmed.
>
> *Physical sensations*: stressed/panicky, tense, headache, gut pain, need to open bowels.
>
> *Behaviour (or 'Actions')*: rushing, snapping at others.

Having carved up these different elements, it's important to recognise that they are not totally independent.

The *physical sensation* of needing to open her bowels is clearly linked to the *thought* 'I need the toilet'. The *emotion* of being annoyed is tied up with the *behaviour* of shouting at Geoff and Alfie, which leads to the *emotion* of guilt. In fact, what we find is any element of this picture (thoughts, emotions, physical sensations, behaviour) can be accompanied by other elements. In some cases it's simply one of them causing the other, but often several are influencing each other all at the same time, so it becomes almost meaningless to say which caused which.

It's actually a bit clearer if we represent all these elements influencing each other in a diagram (Figure 2.1).

This view of how these five areas of experience (context, thoughts, emotions, physical sensations and actions) fit together is common to many forms of CBT,[15] and the original version of this diagram was developed in 1986 by Christine Padesky and Kathleen Mooney.[16] Over time, it has come to be known as the 'hot cross bun', for reasons that may be obvious – to UK readers at least.

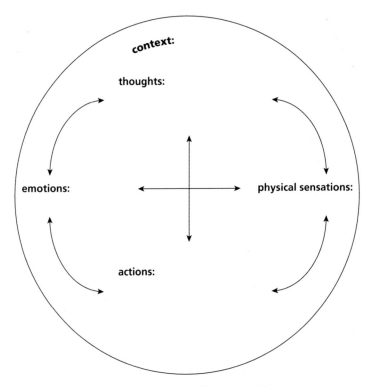

Figure 2.1 'Hot cross bun' model of how people react

I want, though, to emphasise a couple of different things about it to what you'll find in some CBT texts. One form of CBT (Cognitive Therapy)[17] focuses particularly on the 'thoughts' element, and views them as being the 'cause' of the feelings, of the physical sensations or the behaviour. Indeed, some would go so far as to say that the outside world only really affects those other experiences through the thoughts – much as Shakespeare said in *Hamlet*: 'there is nothing either good or bad, but thinking makes it so.' In this book, we're not going to worry too much about which internal event (thought, emotion, etc.) causes another – enough to say that the situation we find ourselves in (physically ill, or in a crowded shop or a doctor's surgery) can affect any or all of these areas of experience.

And that's why the context surrounds all the other elements; in fact, it's probably easier to say that, if thoughts–emotions–physical sensations–actions form a hot cross bun, then context is the plate the bun sits on. And, as we shall see, in our lives (as in psychology) it's essential that we don't get so lost in our 'internal' events (thoughts, feelings, etc.) that we stop paying attention to what's actually happening around us.

There are real benefits in learning to 'stand back' a little and observe our reactions to situations and events, but that can be tricky to learn. It's easier to begin by learning to observe the reactions of others. To give you practice in that, we'll look at the experience of another of the people we've started to follow. Then there's an exercise in making sense of it using the 'hot cross bun'.

Alina used to enjoy Saturday evenings if she wasn't on duty at the hotel. Like tonight, a few of the off-duty staff would get together for a night on the town, or in one of their rooms if money was tight.

But tonight, as so often recently, Alina has turned down the invitation to one of these get-togethers.

Her feet and legs are painful and it doesn't feel worth putting up with the effort of going out. She feels down, and everyone else will be happy: they'll all be dressed-up and attractive, while she just feels fat and ugly.

So tonight she stays in her flat, eating a few too many biscuits and drinking a bit too much wine, watching TV shows without much pleasure before going to bed early.

Exercise 2.1: Thinking about Alina's reactions

Now look through the description of Alina's Saturday night, and try to identify the context, her thoughts, emotions, physical sensations and behaviours on the hot cross bun diagram in Figure 2.2. One possible answer is in Appendix 1 at the back of the book.

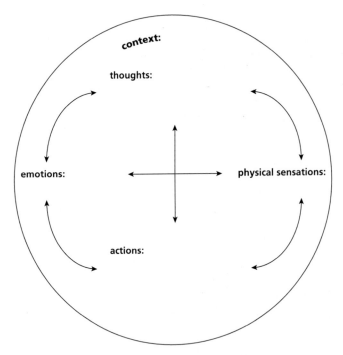

Figure 2.2 'Hot cross bun' model of how people react

It's not that carving up experience in this way gives us some special power over it, but it does begin to introduce a different perspective.

However, Alina's difficulties aren't the real object of this book – it's yours. So the task now – and it will be more challenging – is to do the equivalent for your *own* experience.

Exercise 2.2: Thinking about your reactions

Think of the most recent example you can of a time when you got upset, troubled or annoyed. Try to be as concrete as you can about one specific incident, rather than just basing your answer on how you 'often' or 'generally' respond.

Try to pin down within the episode what was the situation – the **context** – that caused it, what **thoughts** were running through your mind (either in words or pictures), the **emotions** you were feeling, **how you felt physically** (sometimes easy to miss, this one, so really think about whether there was tension in your muscles, a tightness in your stomach, a heaviness across your shoulders, increased heart-rate or similar). And your **actions** – what you actually did in that situation.

And now fill in one of these hot cross bun diagrams for yourself (Figure 2.3). I've put an additional one in Appendix 1 if you'd rather use that. If you'd rather not mark the book, are worried about others seeing your personal responses or are reading this as an e-book, you could always copy one out onto a separate sheet of paper or into a notebook.

I hope you've managed to do that (and if you've just skipped it for now, please do go back and try it – it'll help you to see how the rest of this chapter is relevant to your situation).

It could be that you look at it and feel bad that you haven't managed to deal with the problem better; the chances are that you have at least tried to cope. It could be, though, that those efforts to cope have actually made things worse.

2.2 The nature of the struggle

When things are going wrong, we try to put them right. That comes naturally to us, most of the time anyway. And if we can't fix a problem, we avoid it if we can.

When we talk about 'fixing' here, we're not talking about being able to cure an LTC, but rather to get rid of the stress it creates; not be upset by troubling thoughts or unwanted emotions. The same is true of lots of distress – it's the most natural thing in the world to do whatever it takes to stop hurting; after all, if something was burning your hand or stabbing into your foot, you'd make stopping it a priority.

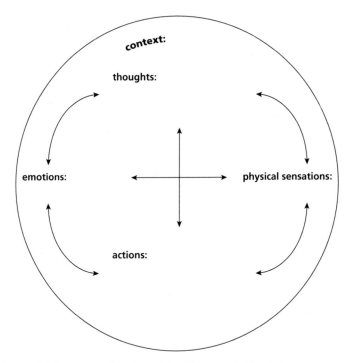

Figure 2.3 'Hot cross bun' model of how people react

The problem is that suffering caused by internal mental events (like thoughts and feelings) is very different from that caused by external physical events (like a hot radiator or a drawing pin in the foot), because the things we try to do in order to stop them are usually ineffective, and often make the problem worse.

There are two particular ways we often approach problems that commonly cause further difficulties, which we can call the Control Agenda and Avoidance.

2.2.1 The Control Agenda (the urge to fix)

One of the reasons Bill has always been successful in management is his attention to detail. When someone had to take over a failing section of the business, Bill's bosses knew he'd be the best man for the job because he'd look at every aspect of the situation, investigate each possible solution, make a sensible choice about how best to proceed, then put the solution into practice thoroughly and with constant checking. The same approach has helped at home too – when sorting out the family finances, and when acting as executor for his parents' wills.

In fact, he finds it hard to be any other way – his wife Trish despairs of how long he takes to decide on a new microwave, or his absolute refusal to 'give up' on a minor fault in the central heating that in reality causes no difficulties.

And now that Bill and his family are facing one of their biggest threats – the possible impact of his illness – his problem-solving abilities are more vital than ever.

Unfortunately, there doesn't seem to be any solution, no matter how hard he thinks through things. He just ends up going round in circles night after night, yet his MS is still incurable, its course is still unpredictable, and the threat to his family's well-being is still real but impossible to quantify. So his nights carry on being disturbed by worry (leaving him tired in the morning), and the rest of the day he finds it hard to pay attention to other things that matter, because his mind keeps returning to the problems that preoccupy him.

Bill's an example of what humans are good at. Compared with other animals, we can't run particularly fast, we don't have armour or big talons to help us survive. But we do have brains that give us the ability to solve problems in a particular way: rather than just deal with a problem that's directly in front of us, happening now, we can instead deal with a problem in our minds.

Imagine far back in our history, a primitive settlement that was sometimes attacked by tigers (or something equally dangerous). At the moment the tiger attack is happening, the resident might be thinking, 'This is terrible – where can I hide? Can I kill the tiger? Can I protect my family?' That's where the faster running or sharp talons might have been an advantage. Maybe during an attack a human can come up with better defence strategies than most animals (e.g. using tools as weapons), but the big human advantage comes *after* the attack, when our minds can run a kind of 'simulation' of an attack, treating memories of and thoughts about the attack in some ways *as if* it was a real attack. Then we can think about different sorts of responses that just wouldn't be possible in the heat of the attack itself: 'Can we make the hut door stronger? What if we dig a ditch around the village and pull up the log-bridge when we see the tiger? Where's the tiger coming from anyway? If we get enough people with spears together, can we track it down and kill it?'

The benefits of this type of mental activity are clear: increased chances of solving the problem. And the same would be true of other challenges too – taking control of food supply problems by developing agriculture, improving shelter against the elements by building better structures and clothing. Having the kind of mind that can address problems that are not currently occurring – reflecting on the past and/or projecting them into the future – looks as if it has huge survival value.

However, it also comes at a cost. An actual tiger attack is probably limited to a few terrifying minutes. Thinking about it – running that mental simulation – can go on for hours or for days. Ideally, once a suitable solution is found, then we can stop thinking about it; but if there's no solution to be found, then the mind can keep churning over and over the problem indefinitely. Even if we think we've found a solution, it might still be hard to stop running over and over it in our minds until the solution has been put into effect, and it's been successful. Most of us can probably think of an example like that – of a confrontation with the boss or a family member that we're dreading, and we keep thinking of different things we might be able to say.

The actual costs of having our heads stuck in this 'chewing over the problem' mode (that we sometimes call rumination, sometimes worrying – there's really not that much difference)[18] are several. It can be exhausting, interrupt sleep and be very distracting – making it hard to concentrate on other things.

The problems go further, though. If you think back to the hot cross bun we looked at earlier, then it should be no surprise that having thoughts about an event is also likely to provoke some degree of the emotional, physical and behavioural responses that the 'real' thing would. So, for example, thinking about your house being broken into might well make you feel more anxious, might raise your heart-rate and blood pressure, and might even make you double-check that your doors are locked.

And because, as we have seen, the repetitive dwelling on the thoughts – in the name of problem-solving – can just carry on and on, so those emotional, physical and behavioural effects can become chronic too, at a cost to your well-being, your quality of life and even your health.[19]

At its widest, the impact of this repetitive preoccupation with problem-solving can be to narrow your life; such is the focus on the topic that other important areas (family, work, leisure, health) may be neglected. Only the problem matters. And, again, for many of the problems that the person with an LTC faces, there simply is no perfect solution to be found, so the process may just go on and on.

Returning then to the case of Bill – our expert problem-solver – we can see how his mind comes to be utterly occupied with the question of what will become of his family as his MS worsens. He gets no closer to an answer, but his sleep gets disturbed and his concentration gets poorer; this means that his quality of life, and that of his family, is being impaired right now, even while he is relatively healthy. That is one of the tragedies of getting tangled up with thoughts about the future or the past; they end up reducing the pleasure we might otherwise get from the present.

We've focused on the way that, when faced with a problem, our tendency to try to 'fix it' can lead to us choosing to spend time on those thoughts. The same can be true of recollections of past problems, where we go back to that argument, that insult, fight or accident time and again. Sometimes there's an element of thinking 'if only I'd said or done this, things would have turned out differently'; perhaps that's a kind of retrospective problem-solving, even if it doesn't really alter anything.

Thinking is not the only way that we can get tangled up in trying to get rid of our problems or the suffering they cause. Our behaviour can become a problem too. Many years ago I met a man whose health was likely to deteriorate in the same way Bill fears. He became obsessed with having his (admittedly rather run-down) house and garden in absolutely perfect condition before this happened, so that his wife and young family would find it less of a burden. Unfortunately, this led to him being so preoccupied with renovation work that his wife and family were neglected – there was never time for long walks or even holidays, because there was always something he needed to do on the house or garden. So what turned out to be the last couple of years where it was easy for them to do 'normal' family things were lost to his determination to make things better for them in one particular way (improving the house). We could see this as another example of 'narrowing your life', and also an example of getting stuck – keep doing the same thing, even though it's not giving you the thing you'd originally hoped it would.

There's another form of control that people naturally try when they're being troubled by unwanted thoughts – and that's suppression: the attempt to inhibit or squash down a thought. The problem here is straightforward; it doesn't work. If I were to ask you to make sure you *don't* think about a white bear for the next 5 minutes (think about anything else you want to, but not a white bear), then the chances are that two things will happen. First, the thought of the white bear will keep occurring and needing to be suppressed during the 5 minutes. Second, you'll probably get a 'rebound' effect; after the 5 minutes is up, those thoughts will keep pushing themselves into your mind.[20] Now, thoughts about white bears probably don't cause people real problems, but it's different if that thought is 'I'll never cope', 'What if the pain gets out of control?' or 'I've failed'. If you try to manage those by suppression, you'll get them coming back more often and more strongly, which is not at all what you were aiming for.

These tendencies we've been discussing – to fix the problem, think our way out of it or squash it down – are understandable attempts to take control, not just of the situation, but of our feelings and responses to it, so that we might avoid feeling the anxiety, or sadness, or frustration that real but unwanted events provoke in us.

And the problem with this Control Agenda is not a moral one – that it is somehow *wrong* to try to be in control of external circumstances and internal experiences at all costs, but rather it's a practical problem; it just so often doesn't work (e.g. rumination actually *decreases* our ability to solve problems,[21] partly by 'tying up' our thinking capacity), and other important things in our lives get neglected in the process. Yet our response to that failure is so often just to try the same thing even harder.

In therapy based on ACT, we often liken this to a man holding a shovel who finds himself in a hole. He wants to get out of his predicament, but the only thing he knows to do is dig. So the hole gets deeper, so he's more desperate to get out of the hole, so he digs harder. He's stuck: not just in the hole, but in a particular way of responding to being in the hole – digging – and that's making his problem worse.

How can we respond better to being in difficulties? Well, that will need to wait for subsequent chapters, because the Control Agenda (becoming over-involved in trying to solve the problem we're facing) isn't the only way we can end up getting stuck and narrowing our lives. Sometimes, we get into difficulties by doing the very opposite.

2.2.2 Avoidance

Alina feels as if she's hit rock-bottom. She's been off work for a week now; it's not that the pain in her feet is getting any worse, but rather that she's just sick of it being there, and sitting or lying at home is less painful (in the short term at least). She hasn't seen any of her friends, because being with them makes her feel inadequate and unattractive, so she tells them she doesn't feel up to having visitors. She could use the time to get on with the coursework for the hotel management qualification she's been doing, but opening the workbooks makes her feel fidgety and bored, and reminds her of how little progress she's making, so they remain unopened on her table. And if she just sits quietly, she's aware of feeling sad and frustrated, so she switches on junk TV or gets another snack simply for a bit of distraction – both of which make her hate herself a little bit more.

It feels to her as if she really can't win, that everything she does to make herself feel better (whether physically better or emotionally) just makes her feel worse.

I know that many people, whether they have an LTC or not, have experienced a situation similar to Alina's: their current situation feels bad, and everything they do to feel better seems to worsen the situation.

It seems natural to talk about trying to 'feel better'. Actually, in these difficult situations I'd argue it's not that people are expecting to feel euphoric, wonderful or 'over the moon'. Rather, they are trying to avoid feeling bad; they just want to stop feeling so sad, scared, angry, shamed, guilty, tired, confused, sore, nauseous …

And avoiding the experience of feeling bad – we sometimes use the phrase **experiential avoidance** – is a perfectly natural response to adversity, just as the desire to fix the problem was (as discussed in the Control Agenda, section 2.2.1). Who would actively choose to prolong those feelings? Very few.

As I said earlier, the problem isn't that it's somehow morally wrong to avoid these unwanted experiences; rather it's that the very attempt to avoid them so often makes matters worse. Consider Alina's example above. To avoid putting up with the pain, she avoids work, but she ends up feeling much worse about herself (and coincidentally probably making her pain worse in the long run – inactivity is often inadvisable in chronic pain problems). To avoid feeling ashamed and unattractive, she stops seeing her friends, making herself feel lonely and cutting down pleasant experiences. To avoid feeling bored and fidgety, she ignores her studies, making herself more depressed about her career.

To avoid feeling sadness, she eats and watches junk TV, reducing her self-esteem further.

Maybe the answer would be to find stronger ways of avoiding the bad feelings? Many people do that, and so could Alina. Instead of the red wine, she could start drinking enough vodka each day to numb all her feelings. Or street drugs might do the same – heroin perhaps. We all know how destructive going down those roads would be.

And, sadly, some resort to the ultimate form of avoidance of bad feeling – suicide. Although that can happen for many reasons, in many cases a person's thoughts turn to it when they find their suffering unbearable, and they see no hope of ever feeling better; indeed, it's been known for a long time that hopelessness is a better predictor of suicidal intent than depression.[22]

It might be tempting to believe that all we need are more effective ways of avoiding these bad feelings, ones with no adverse side-effects. And it seems as if there's always someone suggesting a new technique, or pill, to take away all the suffering and bring permanent healthy, happy normality.

This may sound pessimistic, but I don't think such a thing can exist. Human history seems to show that some degree of suffering is always present, in different forms and to different extents. Even in times of relative plenty and safety, humans will suffer doubt, worry, anger and sadness.

What's more, lots of the things that you might want out of life actually require you to experience some increases in suffering. Want the exhilarating view from the top of a mountain you've just climbed? You'll have to accept tiredness, aches and blisters. Want the rewards of nurturing a child and giving it a good start in life? You'll have to experience sleepless nights, worry for their welfare, mind-numbing end-of-term music concerts, less free time and less disposable income. You can indeed avoid some of those disadvantages, but only at the cost of giving up on the goals you were aiming for.

That, then, is the issue with Avoidance as a strategy; avoidance of unwanted experiences is bought at the cost of giving up important things – in the phrase I used before, by 'narrowing your life'. And even then, if it works in the short term, it may escalate the suffering in the long term.

No surprise, then, that this 'experiential avoidance' looks increasingly like an underlying mechanism in the development and maintenance of a wide range of psychological problems.[23]

It's not just avoidance of unwanted feelings that can get us into trouble; so can avoidance of unwanted thoughts. We've already discussed why thought suppression doesn't work. The other strategy that most of us will use at times is **distraction**. It's familiar enough – if you're worried about something, immerse yourself in a book, or TV, or get on with the housework so that your mind is less able to immerse itself in the troubling thought. And, to an extent, that can help, especially in the short term. For example, one morning I was waiting for a message from my son about exam results – rather than sit and fret, I got a *lot* of work done! It becomes a problem when used long term for thoughts that aren't temporary. That's when people end up getting frantically involved with other things – anything – rather than deal with the thoughts. I also see many people who overwork themselves every day to avoid just sitting and relaxing, because then those avoided thoughts will push themselves back in, in much the same way as we saw with thought suppression. Predictably, this kind of non-stop activity prevents them from pacing themselves and is usually bad news for managing their LTC.

But, you might argue, most people are reasonably bright – why on earth would they persevere with ways of coping that actually make things worse?

There are two answers, one of which is that, whatever the reason, it certainly happens – you can see it all around you: people on endless cycles of dieting, then putting more weight back on; gamblers borrowing money to make one more bet because they think their luck is bound to change; people who are convinced that even though their approach to their family (whether it's aggression, being passive, buying affection or whatever) has never worked before, perhaps if they do that slightly *more*, it will pay off.

The second answer is slightly more complex, and we'll discuss it in more depth later. For now, I'll just say that we sometimes get a 'rule' in our heads about what should work, and then we can get hooked up on following that rule rather than noticing whether it is actually working or not. And I'm sure no one would be surprised if I pointed out that organisations or whole governments can tend to do the same thing.

As we proceed through the book, we'll see other variations of the attempt to Control and the attempt to Avoid; we'll examine things like losing your sense of purpose, having your head stuck in the past and the future (and so losing touch with the present), getting stuck inside a 'story' about your situation rather than noticing what's actually happening, and feeling unable to take constructive steps to make your life better. And we'll look at what you can do about each.

This chapter, though, has been about recognising how genuine and understandable efforts to deal with your problems often end up not working.

Having looked at how those apply to others, it's time for you to consider how it applies to you.

Exercise 2.3: How you've attempted to deal with problems

Take a sheet of paper. Across the top, write the name of the problem you're facing. Not the name of the LTC, but the problem it creates in your life. For example, it could be 'always worrying about illness getting worse', 'feel angry about this happening to me' or 'feel useless'.

Then, down the left-hand column, list any things you've tried to do about that problem. Examples would be 'keep myself busy to distract myself', 'talk to my friends about it' or 'went to evening class'.

In the middle column, write down how well it worked out for you *in the short term* (hours or days). Examples would be 'felt calmer' or 'got a lot of housework done'.

And in the last column, write down how well it worked out for you *in the long term* (weeks or months). For example, 'stressed feelings gradually came back', 'became exhausted doing so much'.

So, for someone who has less strength and stamina than they used to, and ends up feeling like a burden to their family for holding them back on days out, the form might end up looking something like the example in Figure 2.4.

When you look at your own form, at that inventory of things you've tried, there are several things you might notice; it might have been difficult to define the problem in a single sentence. You might have tried lots of different ways of dealing with your problems, or found it hard to find a single one. It may well be that some of the things you've tried helped in the short term, but in the long term either stopped working or actually made things worse. And even where there has been long-term benefit, I'm guessing that it hasn't felt enough. Because, after all, you've chosen to read this book, so it's unlikely that all aspects of your life are going well.

Feeling like a burden to my family		
How I've tried handling it	**SHORT-TERM effect**	**LONG-TERM effect**
Insist I can still do everything for myself	Feel less of burden because not asking for help	End up letting people down when I can't deliver on promises – more guilt
Keep up with everyone else	Avoid asking for help, enjoy feeling 'normal' for a while	Have to give up – embarrassed. Get MORE exhausted, in bed for days to recover
Avoid activities involving family	Relief that they aren't being held back by me	Feel lonely, isolated, left out. Miss out on family life

Figure 2.4 Example of 'ways of coping and their effects' from Exercise 2.3

I do this sort of exercise with a lot of people I see individually for help coping with their health conditions. Sometimes their response to looking at the list of things they've tried – and tried hard with – but that haven't really helped is to feel dispirited. You may even be finding that yourself.

I think that's a price worth paying, though, for this reason: the fantasy (and I'd argue that it is usually a fantasy) of being able to totally control or avoid any suffering is a strong one. Some would argue that some aspects of our culture set us up to believe that is not only achievable but it's actually the norm to be happy and healthy all the time, and anything else is a problem that must be fixed before we can get on with life.

A frank examination of all the things you've sincerely tried in order to deal with the consequences of your LTC (and exactly the same is true of *any* adversity), and the recognition that they haven't delivered what you were expecting, is needed for you to let go of that comforting delusion – that an easeful and suffering-free life awaits the next technique, tablet or treatment. Or that this book will give it to you.

No, the painful step that liberates you is abandoning constant happiness, or the removal of distress, or perfect physical health as a goal.

And have what instead?

A life well lived, even in the presence of unwanted thoughts and unpleasant feelings, be they emotional or physical. Where you address, and sometimes fix, things that are genuinely fixable, and are able to cope with the presence of things that aren't fixable without allowing them to derail you from living the kind of life that matters to you.

That's a lot to take on board in one paragraph; it is, in essence, the philosophy of the ACT approach that this book will be teaching you. But its meaning, relevance, usefulness and achievability will only really become apparent as we proceed.

Key points

- Life with an LTC can have a huge impact physically, practically and psychologically.

- CBT gives us one way of making sense of this impact, by considering the effect of the situation (or context) on thoughts, emotions, physical sensations and behaviour (or actions).
- When we find ourselves suffering unwanted experiences (thoughts, emotions, physical sensations), we have a natural drive to get rid of them either by controlling them or avoiding them; however, both approaches often get us into even more difficulty.
- The urge to control (the Control Agenda) may work well for us in some areas of life, and may have had survival benefits in the past. But faced with a significant problem that is largely uncontrollable (and often unpredictable), we can get stuck in thinking over and over the problem – ruminating or worrying.
- The urge not to feel bad (Avoidance) is a powerful one, and we all do it some of the time.
- Avoidance of unwanted thoughts and emotions can lead to self-destructive behaviours involving alcohol, overeating, drug use or even suicide.
- Avoidance can also lead to us stopping doing things that involve bad feelings, and so we end up missing out on some things that matter to us because of how they make us feel ('narrowing our lives').
- Attempting to suppress unwanted thoughts usually has the effect of making them occur more often.
- Using distraction as a long-term approach for dealing with unwanted thoughts and feelings can cause far more problems than it solves.
- Both Control and Avoidance can sometimes bring short-term relief, but add to problems in the long term.
- Living well with an LTC will involve tackling those things that can be improved *and* learning to accept the presence of things that can't be improved, without getting trapped by the Control Agenda or the urge to Avoid.

3

Troubling thoughts

No one could argue that Caroline doesn't have a lot on her plate. Aside from her own bowel problems, childcare for a lively grandson and supporting her elderly mother, she's also carer for her husband Geoff since his brain injury. Not that he sees it that way – he rarely remembers his limitations and genuinely believes himself to be pretty much capable of everything he was before the accident.

Actually, Caroline has never been afraid of hard work, and years of working with children demonstrate how patient she can be. 'So what's changed now?' she wonders this evening after losing her temper yet again.

Thinking back over the day, it wasn't the effort as such that got to her, and nor was it Geoff's demands – she knows he's not choosing to be like this. No, the worst pressure was from inside her head – the awareness of how little time there was to do everything, the worry that her IBS could flare up at any moment, the sense that everyone was relying on her all the time, and that nagging thought that things weren't meant to be this way. Why did all this have to happen?

Just thinking about it was enough to start her crying. Again.

3.1 The nature of thoughts, and how we get tangled up in them

Many people live with personal situations a bit like Caroline's – busy, with lots of people relying on her. Even more common is that experience of 'pressure from inside her head', of thoughts running riot. And when the going gets tough, those thoughts tend not to be gentle, comforting ones – they tend to be scary, or sad, or angry ones.

It would be tempting to tell ourselves that any disturbing thought is an exaggeration, or something that isn't actually true. It's certainly the case that we can be prone to exaggerating (e.g. *'Nobody* ever helps me') or being too black and white in our thoughts ('If I don't get this piece of work absolutely right, then I'm a complete failure'), and with reflection or help we may be able to spot what's untrue about those thoughts, as is done in Cognitive Therapy. Although stopping those thoughts recurring is another matter entirely.

What else could Caroline do about the stressful thoughts, if they aren't ones that can be argued out of existence? The natural response might be to distract herself, or to suppress the thoughts in some other way. But in the last chapter, when we discussed 'the Control Agenda', we saw why those strategies can, in the long term at least, cause more harm than good. And even in the short term, learning new ways of suppressing or avoiding unwanted thoughts seems not to work.[24]

To understand a different way of dealing with the kind of troubling thoughts that can plague a person with a long-term health condition, we first need to understand a little more about the nature of these thoughts.

In Caroline's case, and in the case of many people struggling with LTCs, one of the issues is that many of the troubling thoughts are not exaggerated or untrue. Her IBS could indeed flare up at any moment – particularly on a stressful day. Others might be troubled with thoughts like 'This illness means I won't be able to go running again' or 'I miss the friends I had when I was still working'. As we've noted before, LTCs genuinely do impact on people's lives, so when a person is having an upsetting thought, then it is entirely possible that it is true, or at least an entirely reasonable response to a difficult situation.

And those thoughts may come in different types; it's easy to focus just on what we might call 'verbal' thoughts – ones that seem similar to speech, only inside the head. I often liken those to the contents of 'think' bubbles over a cartoon character's head from the comics I used to read as a child.

But there are also more 'visual' thoughts. These can be memories – for example, think back to your schooldays and picture where you used to eat your lunch – but can equally refer to the future. I had one client who worried greatly about the possibility of dying and not being around for her children – but that thought tended to come in as a mental picture, of her children putting flowers on her grave. These visual images can be even harder to argue against, maybe because they are less word-like themselves.

I should also mention a third type of thought. Traumatic memories are in some ways similar to other images of the past, but because they refer to highly traumatic events (typically involving the risk of or actual injury or death), they can act in a different way, and may indeed be stored differently in the brain to 'normal' memories.[25] Such memories can push themselves into your awareness very suddenly, be extremely vivid and include recollection of sounds and smells as well as sights. They can evoke very strong emotions (typically fear), and sufferers will often describe the experience as being as if the event were happening again. Typical examples may be memories of car crashes, assaults or horrific combat experiences, and, when certain other reactions are also present, will sometimes be termed post-traumatic stress disorder, or PTSD.[26] Unless we, or those close to us, have been unfortunate enough to experience this, we're most likely to recognise this kind of experience from TV or film (war movies, perhaps).

Yet exactly these kinds of intrusive and disturbing memories can come about in the context of LTCs. Sometimes the traumatic memories are of the moment of diagnosis, or perhaps of some particularly painful or terrifying treatment event;[27] I've certainly had patients who complain of seeing and hearing their doctor giving their diagnosis whenever they close their eyes.

But the other reason for these traumatic memories in the person with an LTC is that the situation seems to awaken old problems, ones that the person has not been troubled with for some time.

It's not uncommon for men in their 70s – like Desmond – to have some breathing difficulties, especially if they worked in heavy industry and were a smoker earlier in their life. Most of the time, his lung problem is a steady inconvenience and a limitation on what he can do. Occasionally, though, it causes a more acute breathing problem; maybe if he's over-exerted himself, or stayed out when the air is too cold. On these occasions, he becomes acutely short of breath, and it feels as if he has to fight for each lungful of air.

But as if that wasn't bad enough, something else happens at that point: the feeling that he can't get his breath triggers memories from his time in the Royal Navy. As a young sailor, he was aboard a minesweeper that sank after an explosion in the engine room. He became trapped in the lower decks as the water was rising and smoke started filling the air. He was convinced he was about to die, as he would have if a closed hatchway hadn't been opened by someone who heard his shouts.

And when one of his episodes of breathlessness happens now, it is as if he were back on the burning ship – it's so vivid that he's sure he can smell the smoke and hear the water rushing in. He feels trapped. This triggers further panic, which makes him gasp for air all the more and become desperate to get out of whatever room he's in. This worsens the attack further. Eventually, it passes, but the experience is so unpleasant that Desmond tries to make sure that he avoids anything that might trigger it. So he spends a lot of time sitting in the safety of his flat, exerting himself as little as possible.

Not many of us might encounter such a strong problem of intrusive memory as Desmond; if you do, I suggest you consult your family doctor with a view to getting help, because psychological therapies for dealing with PTSD-like problems have come on greatly in the last few years.[28]

However, we are all likely to experience milder traumatic memories or upsetting visual images at times. Those are in addition to the more common 'verbal' thoughts (the ones I compared with the 'think' bubbles in comic strips).

It's important to understand that the occurrence of thoughts in our minds – whether they strike us as unpleasant or not – is fairly continuous.

Exercise 3.1: Noticing what thoughts come

We'll be looking at a variety of mental exercises as we go through this book. This one isn't actually about changing anything; rather, it's about noticing what's already going on. As ever, I'd encourage you to give it a go, even if you're tempted to just press on with what's written after it. Read it through a couple of times before you start, so that you don't have to open your eyes to check what to do next.

- Make sure you can sit (or lie) comfortably and undisturbed for the next 3 minutes or so.
- Close your eyes.
- Just concentrate on your breathing. Don't try to change it in any way; just observe it. Notice what your breath feels like in your nose or mouth and in your lungs.
- Try, as best you can, to keep your mind just on your breath.
- When your mind wanders (and it certainly will), just take a moment to notice where it has wandered to, then bring it back to your breath.
- Keep this up for what feels like about 3 minutes – the exact time doesn't matter, and it is better not to interrupt your concentration by opening your eyes to look at a clock.

OK, so having finished, review in your mind all the things that distracted you – that took your mind even for a moment from noticing what it felt like to be breathing.

My guess is that there were quite a lot of things. Some of them may have been noises from outside, or physical sensations – an ache, perhaps, or an itch.

But there will also have been many thoughts. And that's not a problem, because all I'm trying to do here is help you notice just how busy your mind gets.

And in addition to how many thoughts, also notice what types of thoughts: pleasant or unpleasant, to do with the past or the future, things you can do something about or do nothing about.

Bear in mind what you've just noticed as we look further at the problems we have with thoughts.

As the last exercise has hopefully demonstrated, the mind tends to be a busy place, and relatively little of the activity is about the here and now. In fact, one recent study[29] found that almost half the time, our minds are wandering rather than focusing on the present moment, and that the more a mind wanders, the more unhappy the person is. In the context of coping with problems (such as long-term illness can bring), the reason may well be that when the mind wanders, it typically doesn't wander to a happy place. And many of us have had the experience of fantasising about everything turning out well (someone cancels the exam we haven't revised for, a lottery win removes all our financial worries) only to end up feeling even worse when we come back to reality.

So common is the experience of the mind going over and over thoughts of the past and future that we have a variety of ways to describe it; psychologists will often use the term 'ruminate', while in everyday speech we're more likely to talk about dwelling on the past or worrying about the future.

One explanation for why we are so prone to get stuck in this ruminating mode was discussed in section 2.2.1. One of the key functions of the human mind seems to be as a 'problem-solving machine', and worrying is what happens when the mind gets stuck in 'problem-solving mode' even though there's no solution to be found.

It's worth going into a little more detail here.

We've looked at the benefits of the human mind's ability to solve problems which are not currently present (the 'tiger attacking the village' scenario in Chapter 2), and the price we sometimes pay for it in terms of worry. Actually, this seems to be just a specific example of a much wider process. One of the fundamentals of human mental activity is abstract symbolic representation. We take things, make representations of them in our heads, and then do things with those representations in our heads. It's a remarkable ability really, but we do it so constantly that we don't even notice we're doing it. You can look at a chair in a shop and try to picture it in your own living room, even though your living room is not in sight. I give someone an account of a car accident I had, and can answer questions that hadn't occurred to me at the time just by referring back to the representation of the events in my head. I can think of the meal that I plan to cook later, and answer questions about it that I've never considered before, even though that meal doesn't exist yet (e.g. are the peas bigger or smaller than the potatoes? Would it taste better served with gravy or parsley sauce?).

Within ACT, rather than talking about 'representations', we tend to use the word 'language'. So, instead of saying 'How we respond to events is shaped by the mental representations we have of them in our heads', we would say 'Our language shapes our responses'. That's a slightly different use of the word 'language' than we might be used to, because it's a bit wider than just words; it includes images and other possible symbolic representations, but since we do not as yet have any way of observing these happening in the brain, a broad term like 'language' is probably as good as any.

As stated, the benefit is that we can deal with the language representations in our head *as if* it were to some extent the real thing – I can 'try' the new chair by the table or by the TV, almost as if I were physically moving it around. I can react with disgust to the idea of serving the grilled mackerel I'm planning with vanilla ice cream (not that anyone *is* suggesting that, though some avant-garde chef might).

Under certain circumstances, we can react very strongly to an idea in our head in a very similar way to how we would react to the reality. Your stomach can roll and you salivate to a close-up of delicious food on TV; in a dark house at night the thought of the villain of a 'slasher' movie can make your heart pound; seeing a photo of your grandchild can elicit a feeling of love and caring. And the massive pornography industry relies on the fact that ink on a page or images on a screen (or even words) can cause the same physical reactions as actually being in a sexual situation.

So we store these representations and can react to them. But we don't just store them as individual items; we store information about how they relate to other things. For example, if I told you that

'Anne is older than Bob,
and Bob is older than Craig',

you can then work out – or **derive** – extra pieces of information that I've never directly told you. For example, you now know Craig is younger than Anne, even though Craig and Anne were never compared in that original piece of information, and the concept of 'younger than' wasn't mentioned at all. If I now added that

'Zoe is Anne's mother',

then your knowledge that mothers are older than their daughters allows you to tell me a whole list of things about the relative ages of the four people.

Taking that a step further, we can add **rules for behaviour** into that. Say we have a rule, common in many cultures, that

'younger people should give way to older people (e.g. on a crowded train)'.

Now you can tell me a whole list of who should give up their seat for whom, even though I've never specifically told you a single example of anything like 'Bob should give up his seat for Zoe'. If you're interested in the maths, you can actually answer 12 different questions about 'Should X give up their seat for Y?', even though I never told you a single one. That's as well as the 12 'Is X older than Y?' and the 12 'Is X younger than Y?' questions you could answer. All from the few snippets of information I gave you.

That's the kind of thing that human minds (and, it would appear, no other species')[30] easily and routinely do. It leads us to being able to react to situations we've never experienced before and that we don't have direct information about. And as incredibly useful as that can be, it can also get us into trouble.

> The first time Alina developed pain in her back, neck and legs she was taken by surprise. She couldn't work out why it had happened – she hadn't been hurt or lifting anything heavy. When it was clear it wasn't just going away after a few hours, though, she knew what she had to do.
>
> In her teens, she'd been a promising volleyball player and had inevitably suffered a number of painful muscle strains and twisted joints. Her coaches had taught her that the right thing to do when you got hurt like this was to rest the affected area, try to elevate it if possible, wrap it up tightly and apply an ice pack.
>
> So although this was a new pain, it was fairly automatic to her to rest up in bed each time it recurred, even though she ended up there for a few days, and the pain seemed actually to get worse rather than better.

What Alina did was draw the similarity between the new pain and the pains she experienced from volleyball, and apply the rules she'd learned from the acute pain of a sports injury (rest–ice–compress–elevate).[31] If asked, she might not even be aware of that link, but simply say 'It just seemed like the right thing to do'. The problem is that the right way to handle the acute pain of a known minor injury is not necessarily the right way to handle a more chronic type of pain where its origins aren't as clear.[32] In this case, it could well have been that extended periods of immobility made Alina's pain worse, not better. As I said in the opening chapter, it's not within the scope of this book to offer advice on managing the physical aspects of LTCs; Alina's example is there simply to show how a set of associations and rules in her head led her to taking actions that made her health worse, not better.

So the basic way that our minds work seems to bring both great advantages (flexible solving of problems even if those problems are not currently present) and significant costs (rumination when we can't solve the problem, and taking the wrong actions based on applying the wrong rules).

The problem goes further than that, though, because we're so good at creating these representations in our heads, and then responding to them and manipulating them as if they were the real thing, that sometimes we stop noticing that we're dealing with the representation rather than the real thing; it's as if the two have become inseparable. We call this **fusion,** and it turns out to be very important.

3.2 Fusion

Have you ever been reading a novel, or watching a movie, and for a while lost awareness that you're actually sitting on your own couch choosing to be entertained by ink on a page or images on screen? And, instead, it was as if you were on that foggy moor, aboard the sailing ship or in a far-off land? Then you've experienced something very like fusion: the mental experiences created by the storytellers drew you in to the point where you temporarily left reality behind. That's one of the joys of fiction.

Essentially the same thing happens in daily life too, when we become so drawn into our thoughts that we lose touch with the here and now. Daydreaming is an obvious example; your body may actually be on a train, but your mind has you working out how you're going to use your massive lottery winnings.

But at least with daydreaming there's generally a moment of 'coming to' and realising (sometimes painfully) that what you were fantasising about isn't actually real.

A much more insidious version is when you stop noticing the difference between 'internal' events (like thoughts) and external ones, like what is happening in front of you. And it's commoner than we might anticipate.

When Bill starts worrying about the future, it really takes over. It may start with 'If my MS gets worse, I might end up in a wheelchair', but within seconds there's no 'if' about it; he's picturing himself being unable to drive his car, unable to be upstairs in his own house, missing out on country walks. And, worse than that, of becoming impotent and having no sex life – maybe with his wife seeking it elsewhere and leaving him. Or of her becoming more his nurse than his partner, having to wash him and clean him if he wets or soils himself.

Time spent in these thoughts – and it can be many minutes at a time – makes him feel sad, and scared, and angry about what has happened.

No matter how understandable it is for anyone in Bill's position to think like this, much of this suffering is needless. Why? Because he is preoccupied, sad, scared and angry 'about what has happened', but *it hasn't actually happened!* He's lying in his bed, upstairs in his own home, able to make love with his wife, and tomorrow will shower himself, dress himself and then drive off to work that he basically enjoys and that provides well for his family.

That's not to say his fearful thoughts are groundless – some of them may come true. Yet they're not true *now*. And the tragic thing is that, if in a few years time some or all of them have come true, and his life is so much more limited, he may look back on today – when he was actually capable of most of the things he would want – and wonder why he spent this precious time consumed by worry, rather than enjoying life.

What is happening here is that Bill is experiencing his worries – the mental events that his well-developed problem-solving mind presents him with – *as if* they were realities. Not possible, far-off realities, but actual, present realities. And he becomes tangled up in those thoughts – consumed by them. It's not that he couldn't tell the difference if asked, or instantly come back to the here and now if needed, but for the moment his mind is elsewhere.

This is what we mean by **fusion**: losing touch with the difference between the mental experience and actual five-senses experience[33] of reality – what you see, hear, feel, smell and taste actually happening. Or put simply, not noticing the difference between 'the thing' and 'the thought of the thing'. And this allows us to get pulled into our thoughts, so there becomes no distinction between our thoughts and ourselves. We call it *fusion* because it is as if we are fused to these mental events with no distance or separation from them. It is as if I *am* my thoughts, rather than a person *having* those thoughts. We'll explore this loss of sense of self in a later chapter.

And that puts us into the position of Bill reacting to being in wheelchair, when actually he's still very mobile. Or someone thinking about a thousand terrible things that may have happened to their children while they are away on a school trip, even though all is well.

The big problem with fusion (or 'cognitive fusion', to give its full title) is that, because we forget that we are in our thoughts rather than five-senses reality, we don't realise that we're getting a distorted view of what's going on around us; instead, it can seem as if reality itself is that way.

Imagine I got you to wear a pair of green-tinted glasses. Looking around you, what would you see? Obviously, you would see the colours of the world distorted by the green-tinted glasses, but what you would experience would be a world made up of shades of green – the world would be green. You might consciously remind yourself about the distorting glasses, but your mind would tend to react mainly to the green world you now live in.

If, though, you were able to hold those glasses a few inches away from your face, then the situation would change. Let's imagine that you still see the world through the coloured glass, but the big difference is that you are also much more aware of the fact that you are looking through coloured glass. Consequently, you are less likely to slip back into treating the world as if it were all in shades of green.*

That metaphor illustrates the way we can 'know' that we're feeling a bit pessimistic, or mistreated, or euphoric, and that this is probably temporarily colouring how we see the world – yet when we do react to the world based on that state, we mostly forget about that filter being there, and act as if we're seeing things how they really are.

When you start looking for it, fusion is everywhere. We talked about Bill getting tangled up in his fears for the future. But we could easily have been talking about Caroline going over and over the unfairness of her situation rather than attending to what's in front of her. And I'm sure we've all got some topic that just 'takes over' our mind if it creeps in. Long ago, I worked with someone for whom any news story or bit of pub gossip (actually happening or recollected) about someone allegedly being given benefits that he had been turned down for set him off in a spiral of angry thought. I was in conversation with him (several times) when this has happened, and the effect was remarkable – he'd become more animated as he fumed, but at the same time it was as if he wasn't with me any more – he was inside his own head and would spiral into going over the exact same things he'd said a hundred times before (and probably thought a million times). He'd then almost visibly 'come to' and start making eye contact again.

That person was a fairly extreme example, but the basic process is the same in all of us, and the costs are similar. One cost of this is that we are constantly re-exposed to distressing events (even though it is our minds rather than the real world that is doing the exposing). Another is that we lose touch with what is really going on; the chap I was just telling you about was 'away in his head' when he started getting tangled up with his thoughts. But the same was true for Bill, whose worries about future disability – however plausible, however understandable – stopped him from noticing that things were pretty good here and now; so his fusion was stopping him from acting on how things actually were.

And that's the other, potentially bigger loss that fusion can give us: we end up reacting to what our thoughts and feelings are telling us, rather than what is actually happening around us. That's how old habits and unhelpful beliefs get in the way of taking effective action; the thought (the mental event) that 'if someone's upset you should try to cheer them up' prevents you from noticing the evidence of your own eyes

– that every time you do this, your new partner just gets more upset and angry. When we rely upon previously held internal rules of 'how things work', we can lose our sensitivity to how things are actually working in our environment right now, and so fail to get the most out of our situation.[34]

And if you're trying to live life well in the presence of something as challenging as an LTC, you really need to be dealing with what's actually going on now, rather than just stuff that your mind tells you.

So we've learned about what fusion is, how common it is and how much of a problem it is. What can be done about it?

3.3 Defusion

Unsurprisingly, moving away from fusion tends to be called defusion; not as in 'defusing a bomb', but as in pulling back from being fused with thoughts.

It's not about convincing ourselves that thoughts aren't *true* – some will be, some won't – but rather it's about recognising them for what they are: thoughts – transient patterns of electrical discharge in the brain that represent something, but aren't that thing. A thought about a tiger is not a tiger.

Similarly, defusion is not about suppressing a thought, distracting from it and replacing it with a happier alternative. As we saw in Chapter 2, all of those are unlikely to work beyond the very shortest term.

Instead, defusion seeks to stand back from the thought, far enough to recognise it for what it is – a thought and not in itself a reality. If you remember the analogy of the tinted glasses that made the wearer see a green world, defusion is the equivalent of holding the glasses six inches in front of the eyes – much of the world would still be seen through them, but the watcher would be aware that s/he was seeing the world through a pair of distorting glasses, and could adjust accordingly.

The end result is that, when Bill has the thought that he might end up in a wheelchair, he is aware that he is having such a thought, rather than being plunged into a subjective world of disability.

How can a person learn to do that?

Many different exercises have been created within ACT to help people develop the skill of defusing, and there are references in the 'Further reading' section to books and websites with extensive lists of these.

Here, though, are three of the ones I most frequently use with people who come to see me.

Exercise 3.2: Defusion technique – thoughts on paper

Get a small stack of blank pieces of paper – from a notepad, or rip A4 sheets into quarters.

Now sit quietly and think about times when you have been preoccupied, worried, sad, angry, shamed or experiencing some other unpleasant emotion. Write down any thoughts that you tend to have at these times – that's ones that you have frequently, rather than thoughts you've only experienced once or twice. Examples would be thoughts like 'Things are only going to get worse', 'People don't understand how much pain I'm in' or 'I'm a useless parent/partner/friend these days'. Use a fresh piece of paper for each.

If you really can't identify any of those thoughts, you might need to take a bit longer over it – maybe have a go at the end of each day for a week.

You should now a have a small (or not so small) pile of pieces of paper, each with a recurrent troubling thought.

Read back through them – you may feel some emotional reaction (your heart sink a bit, or a flare of anger) as you consider each.

What we're *not* going to do is judge their accuracy, challenge them, spot errors or come up with positive alternatives (as we might in a classic Cognitive Therapy approach).

Instead, just read each thought to yourself ten times, and each time start the sentence with the words 'I have the thought that ...'.

So, for example, 'I have the thought that ... things are only going to get worse' or 'I have the thought that ... people don't understand how much pain I'm in'.

Then do the same exercise at some point tomorrow, adding in any new characteristic thoughts that you've noticed you tend to have. Obviously, we're only really talking about troubling thoughts – although we can be equally fused with neutral thoughts (e.g. 'spare coffee is kept on the top shelf'), they are less prone to cause problems in our lives.

Keep this exercise up every day for a week (realistically, we're not talking about much more than 10 minutes each time), and then once weekly after that.

How does this help?

This is a fairly pure defusion exercise – it is taking exactly those thoughts that trouble you, and that you will (at least sometimes) be fused with, and gets you into the habit of putting them into context. The fused version may be 'things getting worse', but the defused reality is 'I'm having the thought that "things are getting worse"'. Because we're not used to stopping and noticing the difference between a thought and the thing the thought represents, it can be hard to establish that habit. That's why I'm asking you to practise daily, then weekly. Because that will make you much quicker to spot the 'regular culprits' (those thoughts that cause you the most trouble) and then defuse from them.

Exercise 3.3: Defusion technique – thought spotting

This exercise builds on the last one; you could go straight into it, but it would probably be harder to manage it.

The goal is to spot those thoughts that cause you trouble *as they happen*. Ultimately, the aim would be to recognise them popping into your head as you're going about your daily life, but there's a stage between that we can practise.

In some ways, this is a variant of Exercise 3.1 where you sat quietly, focused on your breath and then noticed the things that pulled your concentration away.

So sit (or lie) with eyes closed, somewhere you won't be disturbed for 10 minutes or so.

Now bring to mind some situation that you frequently struggle with, that's typical of the stresses of dealing with your LTC. Visualise yourself in that situation, and try to make it as vivid as you can in your mind. This may not be a comfortable process, and you might feel the pull to think about something else, but persevere anyway – it's good practice of non-avoidance.

Now sit there, picturing this situation, and wait for one of your troublesome thoughts to show up. It may well be one of those from your pile of papers, or maybe a different one shows up. But when it does, notice it and tell yourself: 'I'm having the thought that …'

For example, 'I'm having the thought that … life is crap these days'.

And each time that thought – or any other troublesome one occurs – do the same thing: 'I'm having the thought …'.

Being human, and having a human mind, you're still bound to drift off the task, possibly quite often. But every time you realise you have, just gently and firmly bring yourself back to the activity of waiting for the next thought to surface, then noticing it and naming it *as a thought*.

Once it feels as if about 10 minutes has passed, open your eyes.

How will this help?

In two ways. First, it's further practice at treating those problem thoughts as what they are – thoughts – rather than what they claim they are – realities. Second, you are beginning to spot the thoughts as they occur. This is much trickier than just reading them off sheets of paper, both because we're not in the habit of thinking about our thinking (a process sometimes referred to as 'metacognition')[35] and because these are the very thoughts that you most readily fuse with – that, by definition, means it's harder to see them simply as thoughts.

Exercise 3.4: Defusion technique – 'thank you, mind'

This builds from the last two techniques. If you've applied them well, you'll have become more able to notice when these thoughts occur to you, though you'll still no doubt get carried away on that train of thought at times.

What, though, do you do when you notice one of those thoughts has popped up? It's really important not to get into arguing with it, 'Well, that's not true because…' – that's a route straight back into fusion.

Instead, simply acknowledge that the thought has occurred. Some would say 'Ah, I'm having the thought that …', much as we did in the formal practice sessions of the last technique.

The Australian therapist, writer and GP Russ Harris makes a different suggestion. Although your mind generates these thoughts that end up with you suffering more, it makes little sense to see your mind as your enemy in this. Indeed, we could even see these thoughts as misguided attempts to be helpful – back to warnings and problem-solving.

So his suggested response whenever you spot one of these troubling thoughts is a simple 'Thank you, mind' – and not in a sarcastic manner – followed by returning your attention to whatever it should be on, rather than to the thought that just intruded.[36]

This acknowledges that the thought has occurred, doesn't seek to suppress or argue against it, and is less likely to trigger some unhelpful cycle of self-criticism for having the thought at all.

So, there are three defusion techniques, building on each other. That's several weeks' work before you get into the third one, so it'll take some commitment. And there are a few things to bear in mind:

- Don't forget what we're aiming for here. It's not about reducing how often you have the thoughts, or how believable you find them; it's about reducing their impact and tendency to shape your behaviour. Behavioural psychologists would say that we're changing the *function* of the thought rather than its *content* or *frequency*. It's true that reduced frequency and believability will sometimes come about if you do these exercises, basically because you're no longer 'adding petrol to the fire', but if you actually aim for these reductions, you're buying back into the old Control Agenda and you'll not get the benefit.
- Defusion only works if you do it. Reading about it, thinking about it, agreeing that it seems plausible are only helpful as precursors to actually doing it. You'll need to set aside the time to practise, defend that time, and if some reason you get side-tracked into doing something else instead, make time for it at some point before the end of that same day. And – for reasons we'll discuss later – don't tell yourself 'I'll *try* to make time for it'; that's how we prepare the ground for giving up. Just do it. And accept that it won't always feel comfortable.

Before we move on from the topic of 'thoughts', though, it's really important to consider another aspect. We've spent time on the way that unwanted and troublesome thoughts (whether accurate or inaccurate) can take over our minds to no great benefit and considerable cost.

But we can't afford to treat *all* thoughts as useless distractions to be defused from, especially if we suffer from serious health problems.

3.4 What about thoughts that we *should* pay attention to?

Although it's hard to keep it up at times, Bill's beginning to notice the benefit of learning defusion techniques. Those same old thoughts about wheelchairs, the uncertain future and his relationship still pop up, but he's noticed that he's far less prone to get tangled up in them now. In fact, his main reaction to them occurring is now boredom.

In the last few days, though, a new thought – or set of thoughts – has been occurring to him. He's realised that one of his daughters, Carly, has been acting a little differently for a while; of course, at 13, he expects changes, but the amount of time she spends at friends' houses has escalated, and she frequently misses meals either by being out or because she says she's already eaten there. When she does eat at home, she insists on small portions and avoids the desserts she used to love. Even in hot weather, Carly refuses to wear t-shirts or anything other than baggy clothing. And now that Bill thinks about it, she is looking rather thin.

Of course, Bill's beginning to wonder whether his daughter's developing an eating problem; he's a concerned and caring parent, and he reads about this kind of thing in the newspapers – one of his friends at university had anorexia nervosa.

Here's the dilemma, then: Bill knows (now) he's prone to ruminating on worries and that he easily fuses with those thoughts. Ideas about Carly maybe developing an eating disorder are (understandably) anxiety-provoking. So, should he simply apply his new-found defusion skills to these thoughts so as not to let them get in the way of living his life?

I think my instinct would be: 'No, he needs to keep an eye on this, involve his wife, watch carefully for any other signs that might support his suspicion, or provide an alternative explanation. He may need to look into these problems, maybe take advice if it carries on.'

How, then, can we tell if a troubling thought is one to be considered and acted upon (like this), or to defuse from and move back to some other activity?

The biggest factor is whether this is a *new*, or reasonably new, thought. Problems with fusion are often greatest for thoughts that have been recurring hundreds or even thousands of times. Going back to that idea of the 'problem-solving mind', these are ones that, if thinking was going to resolve them, it would have done so by now. So, if you've chewed it over a thousand times, the chances of the thousand-and-first yielding a solution are low.

Without getting too technical, there's actually a difference between 'thinking carefully about' and 'fusing with'; you can think effectively – maybe more effectively – whilst retaining awareness of the thinking process itself. We're likely to be more effective at problem-solving if we keep some awareness of the boundary between representation and reality.

So the key thing that says 'consider this' rather than 'use defusion techniques and move on' is whether this is a new thought. Once it becomes, as a colleague of mine used to describe it, an 'old, dusty thought', it is less likely to require our attention and action, and it's probably more appropriate to practise defusion and return to the real world around us.

And where (as in Bill's concerns about Carly) the thoughts relate to matters where someone's well-being, health or safety may be threatened, it is reasonable to give more benefit of the doubt to the thought that pops up, in terms of being worth considering further and maybe acting on.

This is a genuine dilemma for many people who have both an LTC and are understandably experiencing stress because of its effect on their lives: how do you decide whether your racing heart, your shortness of breath or your muscular ache is a direct symptom of your condition or the physical feeling of the stress?

It is even more relevant if you (or someone you love) have a health condition where some degree of vigilance about recurrence or worsening of the condition is needed to get prompt treatment. Just stepping aside from, and ignoring, a thought that 'I seem to have a temperature' or 'There's a lump where there wasn't one last time I checked' could have very serious consequences. The simplest answer would be to advise that you check something like that out with your doctor or healthcare team.

It gets a bit more complex, though, because that vigilant and problem-anticipating mind can sometimes get into a cycle of thinking it spots changes where there aren't any, or interpreting any minor twinge or sensation as being sinister. Then you could end up on the phone to your doctor every other day.

If you have got sucked into that kind of health anxiety (and many people do experience it after diagnosis of a real, serious health condition), one approach is to discuss the situation with your doctor/healthcare team, establish how long it would be safe to leave such a new symptom before alerting them if it turned out to be real, then set a rule-of-thumb: that upon noticing such a possible change, you'll leave it the agreed length of time before seeking help. That way, if the apparent symptom is still there, you'll get help in good time; but if it was just your mind thinking it had found something, the thought is likely to have faded long before your cut-off for calling the doctor. I've used this technique with a lot of people, and it does seem to help without putting them at risk.

We have to be careful in these situations because we are very prone to fusion with threat-related thoughts (as Bill found initially about his long-term future); having a rule-of-thumb for when to consult your GP may be helpful, constantly going over it in circles at 3 a.m. probably less so. Again, once the available action has been taken, if the same old, repetitive thoughts keep recurring, then they are unlikely to be moving you forward.

So, it isn't really a question of *either* defusing from a thought *or* acting on it; we can recognise a thought as a thought, and choose to evaluate it (in the way I've just described) and act decisively on it, whilst holding it in a defused way all the time. In fact, I'd argue that you're far more likely to make a wise choice about what to do with this thought from a defused position, whether that is to act on it or simply to notice the thought and then return to what you're engaged with in the present moment.

There's a further technique that can be useful when the thoughts that try to push themselves in are potentially important ones, in the sense that they might need something doing about them at some point. Known as Worry Time[37] – or sometimes as Thinking Time – it works like this:

Exercise 3.5: Worry Time

Every day, put aside a 15 minute period for giving those intrusive thoughts some detailed consideration. Sit yourself somewhere quiet and, with pen and paper to hand, allow any worries or concerns to come into your mind, and give them a few minutes' careful thought each. In particular, ask yourself whether there's anything you can fruitfully do about that thought today. If there is, write down what you're going to do and when, and make sure you do it (and Chapter 8 has advice on following through on plans). If there is nothing you can do, acknowledge that fact then move onto the next thought and repeat the process.

At the end of the 15 minute period, turn to another activity and get on with your day. And whenever a troubling thought occurs for the rest of the day – unless it requires immediate action – put it on a list for considering during the next 'Worry Time' – that will always be less than 24 hours away. It helps if you keep the pen and paper in reach all the time, then even if the thought occurs in the middle of night, you can write it down, and be certain that you'll be able to consider it at the next Worry Time.

The reasoning behind this is that potentially important thoughts cannot afford to be ignored indefinitely, and the more you attempt to, the more they may force themselves into your awareness (like the suppression/distraction problems we looked at in Chapter 2). The absolute knowledge that you will be giving this thought careful consideration within 24 hours seems to decrease the mind's need to keep re-presenting it to you.

As with any technique, what matters is whether it works; if you try this, give it a good couple of weeks of daily use and then judge whether it seems to be helping or not. If it does help, carry on. I've known many people who have found themselves less troubled by worries 'pushing themselves in' once they've starting using it.

Key points

- The thoughts we have cause problems in addition to outside circumstances.
- Some of those thoughts may be incorrect, distorted or exaggerated; many are realistic responses to living with an LTC.
- Sometimes thoughts can be visual images. In extreme cases people can get intrusive images in PTSD-type problems; these can occasionally be triggered by developing an LTC, and may require expert help.
- Minds have a tendency to wander into the past and the future, and we can also end up going over and over thoughts – ruminating. Both things can cause additional suffering.
- The way we represent the world in our heads allows flexible problem-solving, but it also means that thoughts and memories can keep causing problems even when the realities they represent are not present.
- We get so caught up in the content of thoughts that we stop noticing they are actually thoughts, not realities – this is called **cognitive fusion**.
- Cognitive fusion can mean we're reacting to what our thoughts and feelings are telling us, rather than what's actually going on around us; so we can get stuck responding by using out-of-date rules and habits, rather than what actually works now.
- We can learn to defuse from thoughts by recognising that's what we need to do, then undertaking practice exercises and applying in daily life the skills we've now practised.
- Some thoughts require our attention and we need to act on them, particularly where safety or health is concerned. These will typically be new thoughts and things we've just

noticed, rather than old familiar thoughts we've had a thousand times.

- If you are prone to thinking you have spotted signs of serious worsening or recurrence of your condition, and are either worrying excessively or constantly visiting your doctor, you may need to establish a 'rule-of-thumb' for handling the situation, such as the one outlined in the last few paragraphs of this chapter.
- It isn't a choice between defusing from a thought or acting upon it. Even the most accurate, important and action-requiring thought can be held in a defused way, and we're likely to react more flexibly by doing so.
- If potentially important thoughts keep intruding, try the 'Worry Time' technique for managing them.

Note

* And, by the way, anyone thinking the example is too implausible clearly hasn't had my experience of complaining that the low levels of lighting in a restaurant were making it hard to read the lunch menu, only to be told that I'd forgotten to take off my sunglasses.

Unwanted feelings

4.1 The nature of feelings

Feelings can be powerful: sometimes wonderful and sometimes horrible. And, particularly with those feelings that are unwanted, they can at times dominate our lives.

What, for our current purposes, do I mean by feelings? 'Feel' is an interesting word to be using, as it can, in English, be used both to refer to emotional states (e.g. 'I feel sad', 'I feel happy') and to physical ones ('I feel cold', 'I feel queasy'). I think this overlap is useful for how we're going to approach problems here. I won't, however, be using it in the sense of 'I feel that quitting this job is my only option'; although that use of 'feel' is fairly common, I'd argue that this is really another way of saying 'I think', and here we need to distinguish between thoughts and feelings.

There is a huge range of emotional feelings that people experience, describe or write about. Indeed, finding new ways of describing and communicating emotional states seems to be one of the cornerstones of creative writing.[38] As with much language, it's essential that we remember that people may be describing subtly different things using the same word; that's true of all of us, and especially so if we're comparing what a popular newspaper column might mean by a word like 'depressed' (e.g. feeling sad) with how someone working on a psychiatric ward might use the word (e.g. someone who has a range of symptoms that meet the criteria for a formal diagnosis of one of the types of depression listed in a diagnostic manual).

Rather than just launch into a list of words for emotional feelings, I think it makes more sense to consider 'clusters' of emotions, or variants of emotions.

So, we have a 'fear' cluster, involving fear itself, but also its variants like anxiety, concern, terror and panic. These (and many more you could find in any thesaurus) are not interchangeable words; most people would recognise 'concern' as less intense than 'terror', and 'panic' usually has some suggestion of physical symptoms about it (e.g. heart pounding, sweating). They do share similar subjective qualities in having a fear component, and are often triggered by some threat, real or perceived.

There's also a 'sadness' cluster, where people will use words like feeling sad, low, blue, despairing, morose, melancholic and many others. Again, each has its own 'flavour', but they share a similar subjective experience we can label 'sadness', and are often linked to loss or to things not turning out how we would want.

Then there is the 'anger' cluster, including states we might describe as rage, fury, irritation, frustration and so on. Again, these different words imply different specific experiences, but with some degree of anger as a common thread, and are often prompted by some (perceived or real) threat or injustice.

Fear, sadness and anger are often seen as the three main unpleasant emotional states, and certainly, in supporting people who are suffering, they're the ones that social, health and mental health services are most often focused upon.

However, there are other powerful unpleasant emotional feelings that we can (almost all) experience – shame, embarrassment, guilt, disgust. And that's not to mention some more complex combinations of feelings with certain types of thoughts, leading to states such as hopelessness, self-loathing and loneliness.

Before we finish our overview of the range of emotional feelings, it's important to remember that there are also states that people typically consider far more positive: happiness (alongside joy, contentment, euphoria). And, maybe most complex of all, love.

I've talked so far about the emotional feelings that we describe in these ways, and most of us would be able to label our feelings as 'angry', 'sad' and so on, at least most of the time. The unfortunate minority who can't (it's called 'alexithymia' – the inability to read one's own emotions) are at a real disadvantage in coping with everyday life.[39]

I mentioned above that there were benefits to using the word 'feelings' rather than simply 'emotions', principally due to the overlap with 'physical sensations'. People's experiences are different, so I will talk personally here; for me, part of 'feeling sad' is a sensation of heaviness across the shoulders and – especially if very sad, after a bereavement, say – an empty feeling in the middle of the chest. If anxious, I feel the classic 'butterflies in the stomach' sensation and a restlessness in my hands that leads me to fidget. Anger gives a tightness across my chest and in my jaw and – I'm told – I blink more.

Those sensations will vary somewhat depending on the circumstance and how strongly I feel the emotion. I wouldn't expect your experience to be identical, but I would expect that if you examine your experiences closely enough, there would be some physical sensations that form part of your experience of that emotional state.

We could take time to look at how some of those sensations come about – the secretion of hormones like adrenaline and cortisol, the activities of different parts of the nervous system, the consequences of both on circulation, muscular and digestive systems, and the concept of the 'fight, flight or freeze response'.[40] But, in a sense, that doesn't help much, because we're pretty much stuck with the systems we've got.

We do need, however, to consider the overlap between those physical sensations that arise in (most) people's experiences of an emotional state and those that arise directly due to long-term physical health conditions.

It seems to Desmond that almost anything can make his breathing worse these days – a day that's too cold, overdoing things, even standing up too fast seems to do it. Even if flashbacks to nearly dying in the Navy are rare, he does get a little more out of breath if he's generally stressed, such as if he gets worried about the bills, or he's getting hassle off his family or his doctor about needing more help. And especially if people start dropping hints about going into an old people's home.

Things like that can make him worked up for ages, and then he notices that he's shorter of breath. The problem is, his doctor keeps telling him that if he notices his breathing is getting worse, he has to phone for an appointment quickly, because it might actually be the first sign of a chest infection. And, in Desmond's condition, that could be really serious.

When that happens, he doesn't know whether he should be phoning for help or just calming down.

Desmond's dilemma, then, is this: if his breathing gets worse, is that stress that he needs to ignore, or an infection that he has to act on quickly? And, to complicate matters further, it could, of course, be both; if he actually is getting physical problems, then that could be scary enough to give him anxiety-related breathlessness, which would itself make him struggle more for breath. This is often called a 'vicious circle' problem, and can happen for other symptoms too, especially cardiac ones such as increased heart rate.

Having looked at others' emotions, particularly as relates to their physical health problems, it's worthwhile to turn to your own. This next exercise is a starting point for that.

Exercise 4.1: What feelings show up?

This exercise builds on the way we started to recognise thoughts before, but instead focuses on the feelings that show up. Again, read the instructions through a couple of times before you start, so you won't have to open your eyes.

Settle yourself comfortably, sitting or lying, somewhere you won't be disturbed for the next 10 minutes or so.

Start by thinking about your health condition. It could be any aspect of it – how you feel physically on a bad day, any ways that it limits your life or that of your family, or memories of diagnosis and treatment. It could even be any worries you have about your future.

After you've done that for a couple of minutes, start paying attention to whatever emotional **feelings** are present. They might only be small, but pay attention to whatever bits of anxiety, or sadness, or anger, or any other emotion is present. Even if you can't notice any of those, and feel frustrated or bored, then those are kinds of emotion too, so pay attention to them.

Try now to observe that emotional state carefully, as if you were the first person to discover it. Exactly what does it feel like? Where do you feel it most? As well as a general sense of being 'sad' or 'anxious', what are the physical feelings attached to it; where are the limits of that feeling? Are they constant or changing?

After 10 minutes of doing this, open your eyes and think back to your experience. Did it seem typical of how you experience that emotion? What about other emotions you're prone to but which didn't show up in this particular exercise; how do they feel?

So as not to lose the benefit of what you've just observed, it's worth writing down the results.

Take a sheet of blank paper (or use Figure A1.6 in Appendix 1) and draw up four columns labelled as in Figure 4.1. Then write in the name of the emotion you experienced and what physical sensations you noticed. And then make a note of the situation you were thinking about, which made an emotion show up. For instance, if Caroline – the lady we've been following with the IBS and the husband with the brain injury – was doing this exercise, she might write as follows:

Date/ time	Name of emotion	Physical sensations noticed	Situations occurs in
26 Feb, 3.30 p.m.	Anxiety	Knot in stomach, tension across shoulders, sweaty	When I think I'm going to be late for something important

Figure 4.1 Diary of emotions – example

Of course, during one imagination-based exercise, you're unlikely to get a detailed picture of the full range of emotions that show up for you in daily life.

So the second part of this exercise is to turn it into a daily diary. Not a free-form record of your experiences (though those can be useful too in some ways), but in effect a running version of the table we've just done.

At the end of each day, reflect carefully on any situations you found at all stressful or emotional – whether that's as big as receiving bad news, or as small as being irritated by something on TV. In most of our lives there'll be at least one thing each day that makes us at least a little irritated, worried, sad or embarrassed. Or indeed happy – that's an emotion that deserves noticing just as much as the less pleasant ones.

If you remember the first exercise we did in section 2.1 – the hot cross bun – then you might recognise that here we're basically 'zooming in' on the **emotions** and **physical sensations** elements of that diagram.

I'm not suggesting you put this book aside for a full week until you've finished the task, by the way; it'll be useful to carry on becoming more aware of your emotional responses while you're learning what to do with them.

And 'what to do with them' is what we turn to next.

4.2 The urge to control feelings (or, 'Return of the Control Agenda')

If something feels bad, we want to get rid of it, or get away from it; it's understandable. That's what we'd do if something was causing us physical pain – say there was a thorn in your foot, or your hand was on a hot radiator, then you'd want to get rid of the thorn, or pull your hand away from the hot surface.

And yet, as we saw back in section 2.2, both of these tendencies (to fix, or to avoid) can cause more harm than good when applied to internal states (like emotions) rather than external ones (like physical damage). On the one hand, they're often ineffective, and on the other they come at a very high price.

They're often ineffective in two ways. First, the very act of attempting to control or suppress emotions can actually increase that emotion,[41] just as suppressing a thought makes that thought even stronger.[42]

The second way is shown by Alina, the young woman whose chronic pain problem is leading her to do less, to avoid social contact, and whose eating to stave off sadness and boredom is making her feel even worse about herself. Unfortunately, her experience is demonstrating the principle that:

> We end up narrowing our lives in order to avoid feeling bad, and still end up feeling bad anyway.

What I mean by 'narrowing' in that statement is reducing the range (psychologists might say 'repertoire') of things that you do. The act of avoiding is a reduction. And, what's more, remember the point I made back in Chapter 2: whereas Alina narrowed her life by cutting out friends, work, self-development and to an extent her health (through overeating), others might avoid feeling bad by adding in the use of alcohol, drugs, self-harm or even suicide.

You may not have gone to those extremes in responding to feeling bad, but it's very likely that you've either given up some things or done things to make yourself feel better that actually ended up making things worse in the long term. Because we all have. And it's worth facing up to it.

Exercise 4.2: What you've done to avoid feeling bad

Time for more tables, I'm afraid. The first gets you to consider the things you've given up in order to avoid feeling bad, and the effect on your life of doing so. Draw up the columns as in Figure 4.2, and then take a look at the examples I've put in – both drawn from real examples I've worked with in the past. Take some time to think this over carefully – identifying these things isn't always easy; sometimes our avoidance has become such a habit that we stop noticing it. Or we tell ourselves that we have absolutely no alternative, or even that our life is better off without those things. In some ways it might be, but the crucial thing is whether we have chosen to drop them because it moves our lives forwards, or whether it's mainly in order to avoid feeling bad.

So do try to identify any ways in which you've narrowed your life in order to reduce or avoid feeling bad. And if you only come up with one or two examples, come back to the task later and see if you can add any more.

Emotion	Things I've given up because of it	What I miss out on because of doing that
Anxiety	Going out to crowded shops	Contact with friends, shopping then coffee on Saturdays
Anger	Don't watch the TV news any more because it winds me up	Feel out of touch with what's going on in the world

Figure 4.2 Ways that avoiding unwanted feelings narrows your life – example

We'll turn now to a second table, because emotional avoidance also includes those times when we do things to make ourselves feel better; not because they're the sort of things we want our lives to be full of, but because they replace the pain with something nicer in the short term. The issue, sadly, is that they tend to be ineffective, or cause more problems in the long term, and occasionally both.

Again, make up a table with columns as in Figure 4.3. Take a look at the examples I've given, then carefully consider what things you sometimes do to make yourself better, and what their short- and long-term effects are. Even if your list isn't long at first, you might want to add to the table as new examples occur to you.

Emotion	Things I do to make myself feel better	Effects – short-term	Effects – long-term
Sadness	Eat and drink more	Feel comforted and distracted by food and drink	Feel bad about my eating, weight gain, sometimes nauseous
Anxiety	Keep myself distracted all the time	Blocks worry out	Exhausted from constant activity, anxiety still creeps up on me at night

Figure 4.3 Ways of making yourself feel better and their effects – example

Hopefully, you now have two lists of the kind of ways you try to avoid feeling bad – your personal examples of experiential avoidance. And I more or less guarantee there are others that don't come to mind yet, because we all do this. Sometimes it doesn't matter too much, but sometimes it gets us into difficulty. Knowing your own examples will be useful when we start looking at the alternative – acceptance.

But before we do, there's one other strategy for feeling better that I want to touch on, and that's a particular kind of positive self-talk, sometimes called 'affirmations'.

This is where a person with low self-confidence is encouraged to say daily to themselves – possibly whilst looking at themselves in a mirror – 'You *can* do this. You're strong, confident and you *can* succeed'. Or a shy person may say 'People *do* like you. You *can* talk to strangers and they'll find you interesting'. And so on.

A few years ago, this sort of thing was commonly cited advice to help people overcome their anxieties or other unwanted emotions; to give them encouragement and some of the self-confidence they lack.

Superficially at least, you can see a logic to it; it's as if you had a close and trusted friend saying those things in your ear. But there lies the first clue to the problem with this approach. If you've ever been seriously worried about not being able to do something (e.g. pass an exam), being told 'You'll pass easily' doesn't always reassure. Or if you're feeling down, being told 'Cheer up, everything's OK really' can make you feel worse.

Research shows something interesting about these 'positive affirmations'. They can actually help a bit, but mainly for those who are already feeling confident. Use them with someone with low self-esteem, and the affirmations simply make them feel worse.[43] And, other than certain sporting or business settings, it is mainly with people who feel bad that positive affirmations are recommended.

Actually, this finding fits with some of the things I've already discussed about how we represent knowledge in our heads. You may recall from section 3.1 on the nature of thoughts that one of the clever things our minds can do is store the relationships between things, and work out ('derive') conclusions that we were never actually given. So, if I'm told that if Bob is older than Craig, then I know that Craig is younger than Bob, even though no one has mentioned 'younger'. How can I do this? Because I already know that younger is the opposite of older – those two concepts are closely linked (we'd say they're 'in a relationship of opposition'). If someone mentions 'older', then the concept of 'younger' is already implied.

And if I get you to say 'success', then the concept of 'failure' is implied (another 'relationship of opposition'). If you're already hooked up thinking 'I always fail', then you're more likely to get sucked into – to fuse with – that version of the thought than the 'I am a success' form when you effectively activate them both by repeating 'I will succeed in what I attempt'. And – hey presto – someone with low self-confidence, having been given self-affirmations to repeat, actually ends up with lower self-confidence.

Another, more mundane, explanation is the mind's natural tendency to say 'Yes, but ...' to anything it doesn't agree with. So the mind's response to 'I can be an interesting and popular person' could well be 'Yes, but remember that party last week where nobody seemed to want to talk to you ... .'

You might notice that this discussion of some of the pitfalls of positive self-statements has been as much about thoughts as emotions; it appears in this chapter in order to point out that attempting to manipulate or contradict thoughts associated with feeling bad is actually just another form of experiential avoidance.

If, then, all of these responses to bad feelings are ineffective or actually make life worse, does that mean we are helpless, and that there is no approach we can take to help us cope? Not at all.

4.3 'Let it be' – acceptance, or being willing to experience

Hopefully, one of the ideas that has emerged from the discussion above is that whatever the emotional feeling that arises in a situation, the things we do to try to suppress it, fight it, get rid of it or avoid it generally make the situation worse.

So the most sensible response is often to stop fighting – not 'stop fighting for what matters', but rather 'stop fighting the presence of that feeling'. Instead of fighting the feeling, we can **accept** it.

I sometimes hesitate to use the word 'acceptance' when talking about strong and unpleasant – sometimes awful – feelings. That's because 'acceptance', like any other word, is a piece of language that has all sorts of relationships with other ideas in people's heads. So, for some people it's linked to 'giving in' or to 'surrender'. That's not the sense in which I'll be using it here. Rather, I'm talking about a willingness to leave that feeling alone – allow it to be present *not* because that's somehow morally right, but because the alternatives (fighting, disputing, suppressing or avoiding) just don't work, or do more harm than good.

We could liken this to the idea of 'putting out a fire with petrol'; if there's a small fire, and we don't want it to be there, we might have the instinct to throw liquid on it in order to put it out. The trouble is, the only liquid we're holding is petrol – it actually increases the fire rather than putting it out. And the real trouble is that once that happens, given that all we have is more petrol to hand, we end up throwing more on in order to put out the bigger fire.

We can stop the fire from growing and taking over – we do it by letting that initial little flame just be there, and not doing the things that make it worse.

By accepting the presence of the flame – by being willing to let it be – we stop it growing and from taking over. So the price for not having the flame take over is that we have to be willing for it to be there in the first place.

Now let's be clear – 'willing' isn't the same as 'wanting'; we don't *want* the flame to be there, but we might be *willing* to let it be because life is better without a massive inferno.

And to move back from the analogy to reality, if we're willing (and able) to allow the emotional feeling of anxiety to be present, then we can make sure we don't fall into the trap of avoiding, suppressing or distracting that will act like petrol on the flame, turning 'some anxiety' into 'crippling panic'. The same would be true for sadness, anger, guilt, shame and any other unwanted emotional state.

Caroline has been reluctant to go to the stress management class that her sister keeps nagging her about. Frankly, she already has too many things to do; how could adding another two-hour commitment on a Monday afternoon do anything other than increase the pressure? Especially given that it means finding someone to keep an eye on Geoff for the afternoon. But she goes along anyway, mostly to avoid more nagging.

Towards the end of the first session, the group members are being encouraged to sit quietly and notice any strong feelings that are present inside them; for Caroline, it's not hard to spot the anger and resentment that's threatening to burst out of her. Anger at being in the group, at becoming the sort of person who needs to come to a group, and at being robbed of the life she and Geoff were looking forward to. This feeling crops up a lot these days, and she hates it; it makes her feel as if she's going to lose control, and mostly it just isn't *her* to feel like this.

Yet, rather than offer suggestions on how to relax and get rid of these feelings, the group leader keeps encouraging her to focus on what the emotion feels like physically, rather than thinking about it. Well, it feels horrible, and Caroline really doesn't want it to be there; she feels as if she'll 'pop' if it doesn't go away.

Oddly, though, the longer she sits with that feeling, just observing it and letting it be there, the clearer it becomes that she's not going to pop; it's still unpleasant, but nothing terrible is happening, and it occurs to her that maybe feeling like this isn't something she has to fear quite so much. It's going to take a lot more practice to get used to this, but today's session has been quite a revelation.

So, rather than this type of acceptance being a 'giving in', it's actually an active choice to allow an unwanted thing to be present, when attempts to get rid of it would make life worse.

How, though, do we do that? If it's been the habit of a lifetime to fight off unwanted feelings and strive for good ones, how does a person manage to simply sit there with anxiety, or sadness or anger present without it escalating?

Unsurprisingly, as Caroline realises, it'll take practice.

Exercise 4.3: Letting uncomfortable feelings be present

This exercise starts off very similarly to some of the previous ones; so, again, it won't work well if you have to keep opening your eyes to check what to do next. Read through these instructions a couple of times to make sure you can remember what's required.

Again, you need to find yourself somewhere comfortable to sit (or lie) for 15 minutes without being disturbed. Try to ensure you'll be warm enough, and that it's neither just before nor just after a meal (so that you're not distracted by noises from your own stomach). Also make sure you're not going to need the toilet during that time (though, of course, with some bowel conditions, you may not be able to guarantee that).

Allow your eyes to close, and then for the first couple of minutes simply focus on your breath; notice what it feels like to be breathing in and out. That might be most noticeable at your nose or mouth where the air enters and leaves your body, or it might be more noticeable in your chest as your lungs fill and empty. If, because of your health condition, noticing your breathing causes more anxiety, just focus instead on any sounds you can hear.

When your mind wanders – and it certainly will wander – just gently bring it back to your breath (or to the sounds you can hear, if that's your focus).

Now, summon to your mind a situation you have been in recently that was difficult because of your health condition. Try to picture it as vividly as you can, and hold that image in mind. If your mind starts to wander off to something else, just bring it back to picturing that situation.

Try to notice any emotional feeling that goes with that situation – sadness, or anxiety, or frustration, or shame. Pay attention to exactly how that feels, with particular attention to the physical feelings that go with it – any butterflies in the stomach, heaviness across the shoulders, tightness across the chest.

And just let that feeling be there – make room for it. Notice any urge to think of something else, or to soothe the feeling or otherwise make it go away, and just let it be there, and keep paying attention to what it feels like.

Carry on observing and allowing the feeling to be there. If it appears to fade, or you struggle to find it any more, go back to your troublesome situation – or think of another one – and wait for another unwanted feeling to show up. And then pay attention to that.

After 10 minutes or so seem to have passed, switch your attention back to your breathing (or to the noises around you) for another 2–3 minutes, and then open your eyes again.

OK, so what did you experience? Hopefully, a couple of things, the first being an increased awareness of how your feelings make you feel – what the actual experience of being anxious (or sad, or whatever) is physically, rather than just as words in your head saying 'I'm anxious' or 'I'm sad'. And the second, and more important, is some experience of being able to allow the feeling to be there, without trying to reduce it, get rid of it or distract yourself. These urges are still likely to have been there, and you may well have given in to them to some degree, but the practice is about recognising that you can just let them be – be willing to let them sit there, or to accept them, even though you still don't like them. There's a table in Appendix 1 to help you keep a record of this.

And practice it certainly is – I suggest you try this exercise once a day for at least the next week, because that way not only will you get better at allowing those feelings *to be* during the practice, but you're more likely to spot the feelings that arise in daily life. And the big payoff comes when you can 'let it be' then as well. And, as we'll discuss in the next chapter, there are good reasons to make things like this a regular habit.

You might be wondering why there's such an emphasis on the physical sensations associated with emotional feelings (e.g. tension across the shoulders, tightness in the stomach) when the hot cross bun in Chapter 2 showed that thoughts are just as closely tied to emotions as physical sensations are. The main reason is that, in my experience, the mind is more prone to get tangled up with, and distracted by, thoughts than with physical sensations. It goes back to the process of fusion we looked at in the last chapter – it's a more difficult thing for the mind to 'stand back' from its own thoughts than signals coming in from elsewhere in the body.

This skill of allowing unwanted feelings just to be there is useful no matter what the origin of the distress – not just for problems that arise because of physical health problems. This approach also works with all kinds of social or more purely psychological difficulties.[44]

4.4 Acceptance of physical symptoms

We've looked at acceptance (or willingness to experience, or 'letting it be') as applied to emotional feelings. Yet it doesn't stop there, because – as anyone with an LTC will know – emotions are not the only unwanted feelings we experience.

Looking back, Caroline has to admit that the stress management course is proving useful. She's learned not to get too overtaken by her thoughts, and not to react to stress symptoms like tense shoulders as if they're the end of the world, or that they're the first sign that she's going to have some sort of breakdown. She can even manage to let her feelings of resentment just happen without feeling the instant need to get rid of them.

It gets a bit more complicated when her gut plays up, though; she recognises that stress can set it off, but whenever she gets that rolling, griping feeling in her belly, she can't stop herself from beginning to panic. She has thoughts that it might get worse, she might need to find a toilet, and maybe she won't find one in time. Just thinking about that is enough to increase the stress.

So whenever she notices the first, slightest uncomfortable feelings in her gut, she reacts with dread and desperately hopes for it to go away.

Caroline's problem points out a common dilemma: is this physical sensation part of an emotional feeling, or is it a symptom of the long-term condition? We could find similar questions occurring for Desmond (out of breath because of anxiety, or out of breath because of lung disease?) or Alina (pain worse because of muscular tension arising from frustration and worry, or because of a fibromyalgia flare-up?).

This is where we return to a comment I made in the introduction to this book: that it is not my aim here to give guidance on the management of the physical symptoms of LTCs; there are too many of them, and there may be specific approaches for similar symptoms in different conditions. Even two people with the same diagnosis may need to respond differently to a similar symptom. Depending on the illness, the situation and the individual, the best response to pain may be rest or movement; the best response to fatigue may be rest or activity. There can't be universal rules for that kind of management.

This creates a dilemma for the individual trying to make sense of the overlap between the physical reactions to emotional states and the direct physical symptoms of the LTC itself, or indeed treatment side-effects. I believe the wisest response to this is to consult those you trust most about the condition itself; maybe that's your GP, or maybe there's a specialist nurse for your condition or, if you're lucky, a wider support team. It may also be a patient support organisation or website, though, of course, you need to make sure that you are getting sound advice based on evidence (sadly, there is a lot of useless and/or dangerous advice out there). And the two questions you want them to answer are these:

1 Does this physical feeling I experience look like a symptom of the condition, an aspect of emotional state, or could it be either/both?
2 If it did turn out to be an illness symptom, is it one that requires immediate action (e.g. an urgent doctor's appointment, calling an ambulance)? Basically, am I endangering my health if I learn to tolerate its presence?

In a lot of cases, the answers – especially to question 2 – might be reasonably clear-cut. For example, in many chronic pain problems, there is no new damage, no new emergency, whereas for some cardiac conditions, sudden increases in chest tightness and pain might require self-administered medication or urgent medical attention.

Sometimes, even the most expert and supportive advisors can't give you an absolutely black-and-white answer to those questions, but anything they can offer will help you make a more informed decision about whether you are prepared to react to these physical symptoms with acceptance. And, as a 'back-up', you can have a plan for if and when you would check out any new or altered symptoms with your GP or healthcare team (as we discussed in section 3.4).

Subject to those precautions, then, you could indeed practise the same approach of 'letting it be' towards unwanted physical, LTC-related feelings. That would include doing practices like the one above (Exercise 4.3) repeatedly, and learning to notice the urge to distract yourself or to make the symptom better or less, and come back to detached observation of its location, size and characteristics.

This absolutely isn't an easy road to travel. To take the example of long-term pain problems – like Alina's fibromyalgia – the very purpose of acute pain seems to be to alert the attention and focus our behaviour on getting rid of it, so it isn't surprising that chronic pain has a strong tendency to do the same. You may even find that, initially while you are learning to pay attention to the presence of the pain in order to 'let it be', it seems bigger simply because you're not trying to avoid thinking about it and you're choosing to put it centre-stage in your awareness for these minutes. As with feelings that are more simply part of emotions, the aim is not primarily to reduce the experience of the feeling, but rather to reduce the extent to which it dominates your life. And the research evidence that it can work in chronic pain conditions has been independently assessed as 'strong' by the American Psychological Association's register of research-supported treatments.[45]

So, how would this apply in Caroline's case?

At one meeting of the stress management course, Caroline got talking to Jane, who also suffered from IBS. Caroline was describing how quickly she went from noticing the slightest disturbance in her gut to being hugely stressed by the thought of what might happen next.

Jane said she had been exactly the same, and though she suspected that it was the very act of 'worrying what might happen next' that made the symptoms worse, she just hadn't known what to do about it.

However, she'd been using the same 'let it be' exercise that Caroline had learned to use for her anger and resentment with her gut pain. She found that if she paid attention to the actual physical sensations, and let the thoughts about 'It might get worse' or 'I might not reach a toilet in time' simply sit there, without paying much attention to them, then something good happened: it wasn't that the feeling suddenly vanished (more's the pity), but it certainly stopped growing, and the worries didn't escalate. Now, after only a few weeks of trying this, her reaction to the first twinges of gut discomfort were no longer 'Oh no, this is going to end badly', but more like 'This again, eh? Oh well, just need to make room for it.' And there had certainly been fewer times when it had escalated.

Caroline thought that would definitely be worth trying.

4.5 The urge to feel better

You may have noticed a potential paradox – or maybe a trap – that lurks here. If you try to get rid of the unwanted experience (fix it, suppress it, avoid it), it gets worse; when we stop that struggle, we also stop adding petrol to the flames, so the bad feelings aren't as bad. But surely, then, that's exactly the kind of 'trying to get rid of' that we've said causes the problem in the first place?

It's true that if we use these techniques as part of striving to feel better, they're likely to be unsuccessful. And it's so very, very human to want to feel better.

Perhaps the best metaphor here is 'the soap in the bath'; if you want to hold a bar of wet soap in your wet hands, you'd better learn to hold it lightly, because the tighter you grip it, the more surely it's going to squirt out of your hands.

So when you do notice feeling a bit better because you've stopped making things worse by fixing on, suppressing or avoiding your experience, just notice the urge to feel even better, and let that thought just sit there, in the way we discussed in the last chapter.

Some of my more purist colleagues would argue that if we base our actions on reducing our suffering at all, then we are on a slippery slope. Personally, I think that's a big leap for most people to make. Instead, I'd suggest that when we consider these troubling thoughts and unwanted feelings, then we CAN have *less* IF we accept *some*. We can reduce a fire if we accept there being a flame. We can reduce how often we panic if we accept the presence of some anxiety. We can reduce self-loathing depression if we accept the presence of some sadness. We can decrease our angry outbursts if we accept the presence of irritation. And so on. We just have to be careful we're not getting sucked back into 'wanting the bad feelings to go away'.

And what about other things that aim to reduce our unwanted suffering – techniques of relaxation, of soothing ourselves or being soothed, or of medication such as anti-anxiety drugs?

In the final analysis, these too can be seen as part of that Control Agenda that can so often just lead us into more difficulty. The tense person desperately trying to do relaxation exercises, getting more and more stressed. The person taking an anti-anxiety drug that does reduce the panics, but maybe at the cost of feeling more detached and cut off from the world, and with the thought that 'I can only cope if I have my tablets'.

Ultimately, I'd argue that anything where the main aim is to get rid of the unwanted thoughts and feelings runs the risk of being at best a temporary relief, and at worst actually makes the problems worse in the long run.

And yet the approach here is about pragmatism, not ideology – we want to do things that work. Sometimes a person is in such a bad way that they need a crutch to start off with; learning ways of soothing yourself might help you feel confident enough to then learn to accept the presence of feelings without being too scared of what they can do to you.[46] If being on anti-depressants helps get a person out of bed for the first time in weeks, then it may be an important first step to engaging with their problems in a way that will be effective and stable in the long term.

So, just like an actual crutch is used after a person breaks their ankle to support them, keeping moving until they're ready to put weight back on that foot, if you have to use some soothing mechanism to get yourself started, then do what it takes (provided it's not a type of soothing that just escalates your problems, like heavy drinking or hard drugs). So long as, as with an actual crutch, you put it aside as soon as you are able to work on coping with your experiences rather than soothing them. Of course, if we're talking about medication, work with the person who prescribed it to make sure you come off it at the right time and gradually enough, or you could find yourself with withdrawal problems adding to all your other difficulties.

At a more general level, though, I wouldn't want you to think you have to be puritanical about *never* avoiding unpleasant emotion. If you find yourself in social conversation with someone who irritates you massively, you shouldn't feel compelled to prolong the conversation just because to walk away would be experiential avoidance. Similarly, if you're bored, then trying to terminate the boredom by doing something interesting isn't necessarily a problem; it's a question of the impact on your life. So, if you're bored because you're sitting around not doing anything, then interesting activity may improve your life a little. If you're bored because you're doing a piece of work that, though dull, is vital for your job and earning for your family, then you'd be better off not avoiding the boredom but instead learning to accept its presence in the service of feeding your family. It's when the avoidance of discomfort (like boredom or frustration) is in charge of your behaviour that you're in trouble.

4.6 Living with the enemy

I've used the word 'acceptance' at times in this chapter, and pointed out the sense in which I'm using it: not simply accepting the situation for what it is and giving up on changing it, but rather accepting that *at this moment* I am experiencing whatever I am experiencing, and letting it be there (or being willing to have it, or tolerating it), either because fighting that emotion or sensation will simply make things worse, or because this experience is the price you pay for doing something that really matters to you – for example, being willing to experience this anxiety if that's what it takes to stand up and give a speech at a friend's wedding. We'll look at that concept a lot more in the later chapters of this book.

This takes us back to the title of this whole book – that in learning to make the best of life with a serious long-term health problem, we cannot afford to be constantly at war with our own bodies and minds. Neither can we delude ourselves that the health condition is somehow our friend and that we're happy to have pain, fatigue, dizziness, movement restriction or whatever else it brings. No, the task is to learn to live with the enemy, to co-exist even if it still remains your enemy, because that way you don't spend as many of your limited resources on fighting an unwinnable war.

And being able to defuse from troubling thoughts, and let unwanted feelings just be are two of the main tools for managing to co-exist with that enemy. And there are more.

Key points

- Emotional feelings can be powerful elements in our lives, whether wanted or unwanted.
- There is a huge number of words describing particular states; these often belong to 'clusters' or related states, such as anger, sadness, fear, shame, guilt and happiness.
- Emotional feelings have their own physical feelings, but these may also overlap with the physical symptoms of LTCs.
- There is a strong urge to avoid feeling bad, or control any unwanted feelings that do show up; however, doing so causes more problems than it solves.

- We can end up narrowing our lives in the (failed) attempt to avoid feeling bad.
- Striving to 'think positively', including self-affirmations, often makes struggling people feel worse, because they evoke those 'negative' beliefs that they are trying to defeat.
- Rather than trying to fight unwanted feelings, we can practise accepting their presence or letting them be.
- Accepting these feelings is not 'giving in'; it is choosing not to add to their strength by making them the centre of a struggle.
- We can apply the same strategy to many of the physical symptoms of LTCs, *provided* we have a plan in place to make sure we don't ignore potentially dangerous new symptoms.
- Sometimes, emotional feelings may be so extreme that it seems impossible to learn to accept them as they are. If you need to use other 'soothing' techniques to start down the road to acceptance, that may be OK, so long as you are moving towards letting go of them.

5

Living in the present

Though Desmond prefers to spend most of his time in his flat, every Sunday his daughter Mary takes him first to church, then to a family dinner at her house. That was the pattern even when Desmond's wife was still alive. He actually quite enjoys seeing his daughter and the grandchildren, and her cooking's certainly a lot better than the microwave meals he has the rest of the week. However, he also finds these outings tiring and – if he's honest with himself – he tends to be grumpier than he would choose to be.

Driving him back home today, Mary, who's never scared of being firm with him, loses her temper.

'Dad, you're impossible and you're your own worst enemy. Everyone's having a good time – a proper family time, and even the kids stop being sulky teenagers long enough to sit with us and chat. But you just sit there staring into your drink. Half the time I swear you're not even in the same room as us.

'And when you do talk, what's it about? How much better life was when you were younger, the fun you used to have in the Navy; well, it'd be OK if it was just happy stories, but it always comes back to how terrible your life is now compared to that. Or you start dwelling on the worst side of it – the people who died when the ship went down, or all the racism against you as the only black man on the ship. And if you talk about the future, it isn't looking forward to the summer or anything, it's "I won't see another Christmas" or "If I get put in a home, that will be the end of me".

'And today, when I said you were miles away, what did you say back? That you were thinking about the flat, and whether the drug addicts upstairs will have caused another flood.

'What's so bad about being with your own family that you let your head go wandering off anyplace else rather then just *be* there with us for a couple of hours?'

5.1 Why our minds spend so much time elsewhere

Desmond is far from the only person to spend a lot of time with his mind in the past, the future or, even if it's in the present, in a different place to the rest of him. Back in section 3.1, we saw that minds have this tendency to wander, and the more a mind wanders, the more suffering there usually is.

To take Desmond's case, his mind wanders to a future that contains threats of a dreaded move into a care home, or of death coming soon. In the present, his mind wanders to elsewhere – specifically his flat, and ongoing problems with neighbours. Or to the past, where he remembers losing friends in an accident aboard ship, or the racist comments he had to endure from some of the other crew members. Even when he lingers on the fun and excitement of that time, his return to the present leads to his mood dropping as he compares 'life then' to 'life now'. And we can speculate that there were many other examples of things that he was thinking but never spoke out loud to his daughter (not least to thinking back to when his wife would have been by his side at these events).

In each case, his mind is wandering to somewhere that provokes more suffering – either directly (sad memories, frightening future) or indirectly (happy memories that lead to the present seeming even less bearable). Again, this can be true for any of us, but I'd argue that when bad things have been or are happening to people – and having a long-term health problem is certainly an example of that – then more of the places a mind wanders to can be troubling.

But why does the mind have this tendency? There seem to be several reasons.

At the most basic level, going over the past and possible futures seems to be one of the things the mind is for. This was discussed in Chapters 2 and 3; being able to reflect on past events and learn from them (in retrospect, as well as at the time) helps us adapt our behaviour to be more effective. Being able to consider possible future problems allows us to plan ahead and come up with solutions for difficulties before they happen. There are clear survival advantages in having a mind that's able to do this kind of thing. The trouble is, the same processes that can be so useful can also become counterproductive, as Desmond is experiencing.

It's as if this ability that's there for a purpose ends up carrying on all by itself, even when the result is that we suffer more. Looked at this way, the mind wanders out of habit.

And the specific difficulties for people with LTCs come from the nature of their health problems; they're not things that even the cleverest mind can get rid of and they produce uncertain future problems (as large as 'Will I die of this?' or as small as 'Will I feel well enough to do some gardening tomorrow?'). So the mind has plenty of threats to feed on, and very few solutions to bring that thinking to an end. What's more, memories of a pre-illness past may well make today seem like second-best.

I want to be clear about a possible misunderstanding here – it's one I certainly struggled with when I was learning this approach: I am absolutely not saying that thinking ahead or back is always bad – it isn't. Not only are those problem-solving abilities useful, but there can be real pleasure in recollection or looking forward. It's perfectly fine to choose to do those things. But 'choosing' is the key word here, because so many times when a wandering mind gets us into trouble, we haven't chosen to wander – the mind's just gone off and done it of its own accord. And it keeps on doing it.

Exercise 5.1: Watching your mind wander

Back in Chapter 3, I suggested you did a brief concentration exercise. Whether you actually did it then or not, I'm going to invite you again to do it now, especially as it takes less than 5 minutes.

As before, please read through the instructions a couple of times first so you don't have to open your eyes during the exercise to check what to do next.

- Make sure you can sit (or lie) comfortably and undisturbed for the next 3 minutes or so.
- Close your eyes.
- Just concentrate on your breathing. Don't try to change it in any way; just observe it. Notice what your breath feels like in your nose or mouth and in your lungs.
- Try, as best you can, to keep your mind just on your breath.
- When your mind wanders (and it certainly will), take a moment to notice where it has wandered to, then bring it back to your breath.
- Keep this up for what feels like about 3 minutes – the exact time doesn't matter, and it's better not to interrupt your concentration by opening your eyes to look at a clock.

If you did that exercise back when you read Chapter 3, it would be interesting to compare the experience now; it may feel exactly the same, or it may be, if you have been doing the exercises I have suggested in the chapters since then, that you are more quickly aware of your mind wandering. But I would gamble that your mind will certainly have wandered to some extent. Think back over the exercise – try to recall examples of when your mind wandered to other things happening in that moment – maybe sounds around you, or sensations inside you – and examples where you mind wandered to things to do with the past, the future or elsewhere in the present.

We did that exercise sitting quietly in a way that gives the mind plenty of chance to wander. However, as I've already mentioned, it also does the same when we're in the middle of other activities. To show that's true, it's worth taking a closer look at a study I mentioned earlier.[47] More than 2,000 adults volunteered to be prompted by telephone at unpredictable times to answer three questions: how happy they were feeling, what they were doing and whether their minds were on something other than what they were doing at the moment. Although this is just one study, the findings are illuminating; the volunteers reported their minds were wandering on 47 per cent of occasions they were asked, and during almost every activity that was going on at the time (with the exception of occasions when the activity was 'making love'). So, even if you're not just sitting and concentrating on your breath, your mind will wander frequently.

Their second finding was that on those occasions when the mind wandered either to neutral or unpleasant topics, the person was unhappier (and the timing suggested that it was the wandering that caused the unhappiness rather than the other way round). Even wandering to pleasant topics didn't seem to make the person any happier than if they kept their mind in the here and now.

Our first big cost of a wandering mind, then, is that it seems to add to unhappiness.

The second is that, if your mind is in the future and the past for much of the time, you actually miss out on the present. My mother used to tell a story of when my brother was small and the travelling fair came to town; this was a major event each year and was a source of great excitement if we were allowed to go on any of the rides. She remembered watching him on the merry-go-round, and each time he came round, he'd be pointing at another ride and shouting 'I'm going on that one next!' His mind was so fixed on the future that he wasn't paying attention to the ride he was experiencing. When I told my wife this story, she said something similar happened when she was a child; at school dinner, sponge pudding was everyone's favourite, and there was always excitement on the occasions it was served. She recalls once being so preoccupied by whether there would be 'second helpings' that she finished off that once-in-a-while treat without noticing she was doing it or enjoying it properly. And then there were no second helpings. Life's like that.

We can also stop noticing the present if we're focusing on the past rather than the future – I can certainly think of an occasion when I was somewhere pleasant doing something nice (on holiday, having a glass of wine in the sunshine) but my mind was stubbornly back in my job going over an argument I'd had with a colleague.

That, then, is the second big cost of thoughts drifting to future or past – we miss out on many of the good things that are going on right now. That should matter to all of us, I believe, because alongside the bad bits of life, there are good bits too. And it becomes even more important when we are talking about serious physical health problems:

Bill is sitting on a bench in the park staring into the distance, when his younger daughter Rebecca runs up to him. 'Did you see me? I got all the way across, and Carly didn't need to hold my hand at all!' She points back to the climbing frame where her older sister is still standing, waving and smiling at them both.

'Yes, I was watching you all the way,' Bill lies. 'Why don't you see if you can do it again?'

She sets off back at a run, and Bill replays the last couple of minutes in his head. He was lost in thought – as usual. The trip to the park set off a chain of thought about how the MS means he can't play with his daughters like his dad used to play with him. And if he were to have another big relapse, maybe he'll be sitting here in a wheelchair, or unable to get here at all.

And he's been so busy thinking those things that he wasn't really watching his girls playing so well together, and Rebecca's big achievement on the climbing frame.

As Rebecca clambers back on to the frame, he watches very carefully and shouts encouragement. And enjoys every moment of it.

It's ironic – but an irony that's tragically common – that Bill is so busy worrying about missing out on good times with his girls in the future that he misses out on them right now. And not because of MS, but because of his mind, and his failure to notice what's actually going on in front of him. This can happen to anyone, but it's even sadder to see when someone is so preoccupied with future incapacity or death that they let slip by a present moment when they can actually do many or all of things they fear losing.

There's a saying that if you don't pay attention to the present moment, then it doesn't matter even if you're given another 100 years to live, because you probably won't show up for that either!

If these are the costs of having the mind wander, of not paying attention to the here and now, then is there an alternative?

5.2 Present moment awareness and mindfulness

In the search for increasing our attention to the here and now – that we can also term *present moment awareness* – we come across the concept of mindfulness.

Now, I don't think it would suit the purposes of this book to delve too far into the psychological, philosophical or historical debates around how this word has been used. In case you're interested in how it came to be developed from Buddhism and used in Western healthcare over the last few decades, there's a brief outline in Appendix 2.

At the heart of mindfulness is paying attention to whatever is present, inside the body or outside it, in this present moment, and doing so in a way that emphasises noticing and observing these things, rather than thinking about them or judging them. So, as I sit here writing, I notice the feel of the keys under my fingers (and choose not to dwell on whether this keyboard is better than the one on my old computer). Or I notice the colour of the sky as the sun sets, choosing not to focus on whether the nice weather will continue to the end of the week.

The form of mindfulness taught in most Western healthcare settings isn't just limited to this 'present moment awareness', but also includes concepts like treating thoughts as just thoughts (as we examined in Chapter 3), acceptance of emotional states (as in Chapter 4) and the Observing Self (which we'll look at in the next chapter).

We have been looking at these different elements separately and in some detail, and will go on to examine important ideas that aren't a traditional part of mindfulness (e.g. Values). For this reason, I won't use mindfulness in its wider sense, but just as it describes present moment awareness. Or, as one Buddhist writer on mindfulness puts it, 'the clear and single-minded awareness of what actually happens to us and in us at the successive moments of perception'.[48]

And the present moment matters because it is the only moment in which we can really do anything about our lives, so noticing what is actually going on should form the basis of what we do next, rather than old habits from the past or vague fears of the future.

I'm not talking here simply about 'living for today' – we still need to think about and plan for the future, and reflect on and learn from the past. 'Living for today' can be a recipe (or maybe an excuse) for short-term pleasure-seeking, avoiding responsibility and failure to act to improve your future.

What I'm talking about here is rather 'living *in* today'; that the here and now is your solid base, and that thinking about the future or the past are deliberate acts you perform from a position of awareness of what's really here and now. It just means you're less likely to get 'lost' in fears, regrets, bitter thoughts and so on, because you're more able to notice the difference between these mental events (be they thoughts or feelings) and the reality of the chair you're sitting in, the people around you, the food on your plate.

The other big pay-off of staying in the present more is that you notice more. That includes getting more out of the pleasant things.

Since Bill has – reluctantly at first – been attending a mindfulness class, he's been noticing several things. These include just how much of the time he's either worrying, or keeping busy in order to block the worrying out, how tired this approach to life has been making him, and how that adds to the symptoms of his MS.

Yet in today's class, he finds himself laughing; the teacher is talking about how we can so easily lose touch with the things going on around us, and he suddenly finds himself thinking about a weekend at the seaside with his kids the previous summer. The sun was shining, but not so hot as to make his MS worse. He was walking along the beach with his family; the sand at the water's edge was firm enough to make walking easy, and there was a cooling breeze from off the sea.

At least, he realises those things looking back; at the time his thoughts ran something like this:

'I hope the weather stays like this for the rest of the holiday; it was miserable last year when we tried camping and it rained all the time – I couldn't stand that again. People at work will be envious that I got this week off. Suppose I'd better take them something back – some rock or fudge or something, I guess. Mind you, everyone's always on a diet. And they won't appreciate it anyway – probably too busy putting that new financial management system into practice. I bet it'll be in chaos by the time I get back, and guess who'll have to pick up the pieces? Me, of course. Maybe I was wrong to insist on being out of contact while I'm on holiday – it'll probably save me work in the long run if I just give them a quick call this afternoon to head off any problems.'

It strikes him that the very kind of thing he most fears losing due to his condition – a happy family life – he had been throwing away by just not noticing it was going on around him.

Even when you're not having a particularly nice time, paying attention can help you notice that there are some elements of your experience that aren't as bad. In the dentist's chair, when there is pain, discomfort or fear of what might be coming next, it can be useful to pay attention to – for example – the smooth, cool surface of the chair itself. We have to be careful here, though; attempting to block out all other aspects of the experience by focusing on the feel of the chair may well not be effective – remember what we have discussed about suppressed thoughts getting stronger. It helps to notice that *as well as* the unpleasant stuff, there are also things around that aren't unpleasant.

But what if the present is so rubbish that I don't *want* to pay attention to it? What if I'd rather spend my time imagining a better future or recalling a happier past?

I'd take a firm line on this: while, of course, we shouldn't forget the past or give up on the future, you'll pay a high price in terms of mood and well-being for spending too much time in them rather than in the present.[49]

Moreover, the present moment is the only time any of us can act in – putting off action until the future removes the possibility of improving the present moment in even the smallest way. And to act effectively in the present moment requires a frank and unblinking perception of what's really going on right here and right now.

I've said earlier in the book that acceptance isn't the same as giving up on a problem; but I think running away from the present (however understandable the urge) *is* a kind of giving up. And it's not that that is somehow morally bad, but it does increase the risk of being stuck, and can lead to the kind of helplessness and hopelessness that's linked to depression and even in extreme cases to suicide.

And as I've mentioned before, however temporarily pleasant it is to drift off into fantasy (of a lottery win, of a cure for our suffering, of a loved one still being with us), there's always pain on the return to reality.

Enough, then, of what mindfulness (or present moment awareness) is, and why it's useful; how do you learn to be more mindful?

5.3 Mindfulness in everyday life

Exercise 5.2: Mindfulness of a simple activity

Try this.

Get up from wherever you're reading this, walk across the room, pick up some object, put it down again, then walk back and take up this book again.

(If that's physically impossible – either because of where you are or maybe your condition means you can't do those things – then do some other simple sequence of everyday actions that takes no more than 20 seconds or so, and adapt the next instructions accordingly.)

Don't read on until you've done that.

Now you've done that, think about what you noticed while you were doing it – what kind of things were you aware of while you were doing that set of actions? Did you notice *at the time* the feel of the flooring under your feet? The texture of the object you picked up? What sounds were in the background? What could you smell while you were doing it? How did light and shadow affect the colour of the thing you picked up?

OK, now repeat the action, but this time try to pay attention to what your senses are telling you throughout. Start with noticing the movement of your muscles and bones as you get up. Then try to feel the contact of your clothing against your skin as you move. And the feel of the floor under your feet (the softness of carpet, or maybe the hardness of wood). Notice next the object you're going to pick up, and pay attention to any other things around it. Notice what the muscles in your arms and hands feel like as you reach forward to pick it up. Feel the weight of the object. Pay attention to the texture of its surface, and whether it feels warm or cold to the touch. Next, look carefully at it; notice the colours and variations of colour, areas of light and shade, and how smooth or textured different surfaces are. And as you put it down, notice the tiny movements of muscles in your hand while placing it gently and precisely back in place. Turn around, paying attention to the complex movements of muscles and joints in your legs, ankles and feet that allow you to keep your balance. And then the sensations of movement within your body as you return to your starting place. How clothing moves, stretches, rubs against your skin as you move. Then notice the way different muscles and joints work together to allow you to sit back down. And finally take a moment to pay attention to the sensation of the chair beneath you, supporting your weight.

I ask many of the clients I see to do that exercise, or variations on it, and then ask what struck them during it. Typical answers would be:

- I'd never realised there were so many little movements going on in my body when I move.
- There's so much detail in everything around us – I never normally notice it.
- I ended up doing it much slower the second time.
- I was totally absorbed in what I was doing – I didn't think about my other worries at all.

Or, alternatively:

- I found it really hard to concentrate on what I was doing – I kept having thoughts like 'Am I doing this right?' or 'What's the point of this, and how's it meant to help me?'

To address the last question, here's why I suggested you did this exercise. It aims to show you that there are so many things actually happening in this present moment that we simply don't pay attention to, because our minds are off in the future, the past or on other things. We are so preoccupied that we fail to spot what's in front of us.

Now, the texture of an ornament you pick up may not be all that significant for your well-being, but other things you're failing to notice will be: the difference between how your stomach feels after one foodstuff versus another (very important if you have a bowel disorder); how much dust is building up on your shelves (not helpful with some breathing problems); how your daughter reacts when she sees you wince with pain.

Coping well with an LTC (or any adversity) requires you to notice what's actually happening in front of you, rather than simply what your mind is telling you about the past, the future or what it wants to believe.

Present moment awareness, or mindfulness, gets us more able to do that: it helps us develop the skill of noticing in the present moment – and gets us into the habit of applying that skill.

In order to develop the skill and the habit, I'm going to recommend two approaches. In a moment, we'll look at 'formal practice', but first I want to take us a little further on the 'mindfulness in everyday life' that we've been looking at.

In the previous activity, I gave you a specific action to do (move across the room, pick up an object) whilst paying close attention to what your senses were telling you about what was actually present in your experience, rather than in your thoughts; we can call that doing something **mindfully**. The next task transfers that approach to real daily activities that are already part of your life, which you can also practise doing mindfully.

Exercise 5.3: Mindfulness of an everyday activity

Choose an activity that you do routinely every day; it could be showering, dressing, cleaning your teeth, washing dishes, or almost anything that doesn't involve interacting with other people, and preferably doesn't have safety implications if you concentrate differently on it (for example, I wouldn't suggest doing this for driving, operating dangerous machines or chopping vegetables).

From the next time you do this thing (today or tomorrow), and for the next week, do that activity with the level of attention to your senses that we used in the previous exercise. So, if you've chosen showering, try to notice the sensation of water against your skin – where is it most intense, where less so? Notice the smell of the shower gel, the difference between the texture when it first comes out of the bottle and the feeling when it has foamed up under the water. Pay attention to the difference in temperature between areas of your skin the water is hitting or not. Listen to the sound of the shower, and how any other sounds are altered by being under the water. Look at the patterns the water is making against the tiles or shower cubicle/curtain.

Hopefully, you can see how you can bring the same kind of attention to towelling yourself dry, or to cleaning your teeth, or whatever other everyday activity you have chosen.

> And do this with the same activity every day for a week, just to get some practice of keeping your awareness in the present moment.
>
> Then, for a second week, try doing the same thing but with a different task each day.

By the end of that fortnight, you should both have increased your skill level at staying in the present moment and begun to establish a bit of a habit of doing it. From then on, just try 'dropping into' that state for a few minutes each day. It can be a good thing to try while stuck (and stationary) in traffic; rather than fuming about the delay and worrying about the consequences of being late, pay attention to the texture of the steering wheel under your hands, the different colours of cars, vans and street signs, the temperature of your skin. And at times when you're actually doing something enjoyable, then you can get even more pleasure out of it by using your new-found awareness of the experience; so if you're walking on a beach, really notice the sensation of sand between your toes, breeze against skin – all the things that Bill failed to notice at the beginning of this chapter because his mind was elsewhere.

One other everyday activity to mention – eating. One of the standard introductory mindfulness exercises is 'eat one raisin', introduced by Jon Kabat-Zinn.[50] In this, the individual is encouraged to do exactly that: eat a single raisin, having carefully examined its appearance, held it up to the light, inhaled its scent, touched it against skin, felt it on the tongue, investigated how much resistance it gives to being bitten. I'm sure you recognise the approach by now.

One of the comments people often make after that exercise is that the raisin tasted much better than expected, and that this single raisin was more satisfying than a whole handful thrown down the throat mindlessly while watching TV.

It should be no surprise, then, that scaling that response up to a whole meal can have quite an effect upon your experience of eating; most of us might find the food tastier, and we will probably eat more slowly. For those with a weight problem (either by itself or alongside other health problems such as high blood pressure, diabetes or indeed almost any LTC), this can be beneficial, as it means a smaller amount of food than usual is found as satisfying. Slower eating is itself helpful and mindful awareness of bodily sensations makes the individual more likely to notice when they are full, and stop eating at that point.[51] For these reasons, there has recently been increasing interest in mindfulness-based approaches with people with significant weight- and eating-related problems, both from researchers[52] and self-help books.[53]

You might be objecting, though, that you don't want to stay in the present moment all the time – that it's less fun or even unhelpful to do that. What happens to thinking about the past, planning for the future, daydreaming, being immersed in a book, film or video game?

Although some people might take a different line to me (some schools of Buddhist thought, for instance), I'd argue that we're *not* aiming to be fully mindful – our minds 'full' of only the present moment for all our waking hours. All of those things – remembering, planning, daydreaming, imagining and so on – matter greatly to me too, and I wouldn't give them up. However, I'd say that they're good things when they're *chosen*; the problem comes when the mind wanders off and does its own thing, and we haven't even noticed how we've drifted away from the here and now.

We could say that the present moment should be our secure base and our default location – we take frequent excursions but always with a rope tethering us to the here and now. And mindfulness practice helps us to get better at noticing when we've strayed too far or too long without realising it.

So far, this section on learning to be more aware of the present moment has focused upon everyday activities, and maybe that is, in the long term, the place that matters most.

However, many would argue that we'll never really be able to adopt a more mindful approach in our daily lives without dedicating time to more formal practice, so that is what we'll turn to now.

5.4 Formal mindfulness practice

By formal practice, I mean a mindfulness activity that you choose to do separately from your other daily activities; where, indeed, you put aside other activity for a period of time in order to practise your mindfulness. And both meanings of the verb 'to practise' apply here, because you are both doing it to benefit from it *and* doing it in order to get better at it.

There are many different mindfulness practices out there that you can try, in books, CDs and online, and they involve different activities (typically different focuses of attention) and are of different lengths.

While I agree that there has to be more than a token 'dose' of mindfulness for it to be worth doing formal practice at all, I'm also at heart a pragmatist and believe that 10 minutes of practice that you actually do daily is better than 45 minutes of practice that you never quite get round to.

And daily does matter for this – especially in the early stages – for three reasons. First, regular frequent practice tends to be the best approach to any skill, whether mindfulness or a musical instrument.[54] Second, the very effort of finding time, or making time, to do this daily is itself a choice that you have made to do something possibly inconvenient, for a good reason; we'll see why that matters in later chapters. And third, it'll mean that every day has some mindfulness in it, and I'd argue that day will be better for it.

The exercise I'm going to suggest is in some ways the simplest of all the mindfulness practices, though, of course, 'simple' isn't the same as 'easy'. It does also have the benefit of having fewest instructions, which helps with remembering what to do. We've actually been through a shorter version of it before – in Chapter 3 – where we used it as a way of learning more about the way thoughts intrude. Although the procedure here is at heart the same, it will be for longer, and the goal this time is to allow a more prolonged experience of paying attention to one thing (the breath), noticing when the mind wanders, then coming back to the breath; and doing that as many times as necessary.

Exercise 5.4: Mindfulness of the breath

As before, read the exercise through a couple of times before trying, and make sure you've got 10–15 minutes to follow through: with your phone on silent, no one likely to disturb you and determination not to respond to anything external short of a fire alarm.

- Settle yourself into a comfortable sitting or lying position.
- Close your eyes.
- Take a moment to remind yourself of your intention here: simply to pay attention to the breath.
- Just concentrate on the sensation of breathing, wherever that sensation is most noticeable: that may be at the nose or mouth as the air enters and leaves your body; it may be in your chest as your lungs fill and empty; it may even be in your abdomen as it moves backwards and forwards slightly to make room for your lungs filling.
- Don't try to change it in any way; just observe it.
- Focus on the sensation of breathing – what it physically feels like – rather than thinking intellectually about what's going on there.
- Try, as best you can, to keep your mind just on your breath.
- When your mind wanders (and it certainly will – probably many, many times), just take a moment to notice where it has wandered to, then bring it back to your breath, without judging yourself for having a mind that wandered.
- Keep this up for what feels like about 10 minutes or so – the exact time doesn't matter, and it is better not to interrupt your concentration by opening your eyes to look at a clock. If you finish and discover only 2 minutes has passed, simply close your eyes again and carry on.

- Remember, the intention is not to maintain perfect concentration (it won't happen) or become calmer or more relaxed (at most, that's a pleasant side-effect). The intention is simply to:

  o focus on the breath
  o notice when your mind wanders
  o come back to the breath
  o keep repeating this.

- When you do finish, open your eyes, and just stay still for a few more moments before you get up.

All sorts of reactions to that experience are possible; some of the ones I come across are:

- Time passed much quicker than I expected.
- Time passed much slower than I expected.
- My mind was racing all the time.
- There were brief parts where my mind settled down.
- That felt really uncomfortable.
- I feel really relaxed now.
- That was easy.
- I was rubbish at that.

The important thing to remember is that you're not doing the practice in order to be relaxed, or even to have your mind stay totally in one place; you're doing it in order to stay in the present, gently observing *whatever* is going on in there – whether that's a calm mind, busy mind, blissful relaxation or uncomfortable agitation. To step back from it, to notice it, then to bring your mind back to a real, here-and-now focus rather than just following wherever it wanders. You're doing that both for the benefits that those 10–15 minutes bring to your day, and also to develop the habit of noticing in everyday life when your mind has gone off wandering to past or future, or latched on to something that right now isn't your chosen focus.

I realise I've said some of those things a few times before, but I (almost) guarantee that no matter how well you 'get' these principles right now, as you continue to practise, your mind will time and time again go back to '... this should be relaxing' and '... my mind shouldn't be wandering'. My advice is treat them for what they are – stuff your mind tells you; just recognise them ('Oh, you again, eh?'), and then move your attention back to the here and now.

If you do manage to get into the habit of a routine, day-in, day-out practice, then you may well feel the need for some variety. A real purist might say that boredom or desire for change would just be another thing your mind is throwing at you, and the appropriate response is just to notice it then come back to the breath again. However, keeping practice going is the important thing, so anything that keeps you going at it is worthwhile.

In that spirit, here's another practice; it's probably the one I personally use most, and most often teach to people I see if there isn't the chance to go through a whole course on mindfulness. If you read my previous book about dealing with life crises – *Facing the Storm* – you may recognise it as a slightly adapted version of one I presented there too.[55]

Exercise 5.5: Here and now

- Sit somewhere you can be undisturbed for the next 10 minutes or so. Settle into a comfortable but reasonably upright position (slouching could become uncomfortable).
- Let your gaze wander the room until you find something to look at – it doesn't really matter what; it could be a chair, light fitting, patch of carpet or anything. Now really look at it, notice its colour, variation of light and shade, texture, lines and angles. After 30 seconds or so, say inside your head 'Right here and now, I'm seeing a ... [*whatever you're looking at*]'.
- Then move your gaze on to something else and repeat the process, ending with 'Right here and now, I'm a seeing a ...'.

- Next, allow your eyes to close, and pay attention to what you can hear. Select one sound, and notice in detail its qualities – how loud or soft, whether it's constant or changing, whether your mind judges it pleasant or unpleasant. Then say in your head 'Right here and now, I'm hearing [*whatever the sound is*]'. Then find another sound, and do the same.

- Now switch your attention to the sense of touch. Find something that you can feel in contact with you – it could be clothing against skin, the chair underneath you, socks against feet or anything else. Really notice what it feels like, then say to yourself 'Right here and now, I'm feeling [*whatever the sensation is*]'. Let go of that sensation of touch, and find another; same drill.

- This time, find a sensation anywhere within your body. It doesn't have to be significant – it could just be any feelings you can detect inside your foot, calf, stomach or shoulders – and it doesn't matter whether it's pleasant, unpleasant or neutral; we're just interested in giving you practice in noticing. Then say 'Right here and now, I'm feeling [*whatever the sensation is*]'. Then move on to a second. Don't give up if you think you can't find anything to feel inside; at worst, move an arm or leg and notice what that feels like.

- Now turn your attention to your breath; just notice whatever there is to notice about the sensation of breathing. Don't try to change anything about your breathing; just let it carry on at whatever pace and depth it wants to. You might be most aware of it in your mouth and nose as breath enters and leaves your body, or in your chest as the lungs fill and empty, or in your stomach as it moves to make room for the lungs filling and emptying. For a couple of minutes, just rest your attention on your breath. And when your mind wanders – which it surely will – simply notice where it's gone to, and gently bring it back to this breath, here and now.

- After a couple of minutes of this, take two intentionally deeper breaths, and allow your eyes to open again.

- So to recap: it's two things I see, two things I hear, two things I feel (from the outside), two things I feel (from the inside), then focus on the breath.
- Do this daily for at least the next week (and preferably longer).

There are two things I particularly like about that exercise. The first is that it starts with the 'outside' world – things you can see and hear – and gradually brings you back to your breath; that can be very settling if your mind is feeling scattered by lots of external demands. Indeed, a version of this is sometimes used as a 'grounding' exercise with disaster survivors who are in great distress.[56]

The second reason for recommending this exercise is the repeated reminder of what you are doing *here and now*; recognising and repeatedly coming back to the here and now is at the very heart of present moment awareness or mindfulness, and noticing you're doing it helps develop that skill.

You might want to explore other approaches to developing your mindfulness skills. Look around to see if there is a meditation class locally – doing these practices led by another person can be a very different experience. Clearly, though, the exact type of practice you do will vary depending on whether the class is led by, say, a yoga teacher or a Buddhist monk. Not every aspect of the approach might agree with what I have been saying in this book.

There are also other activities such as yoga, tai chi and chi gong that, though not primarily described as mindfulness-based, have a large component of mindfulness about them; particularly, paying close attention in the present moment to the detailed sensations arising in your body during movement.

There is one final objection that I sometimes hear to the idea of spending more time in the present, particularly from people with serious health conditions, or other losses:

'I don't want to spend more time in the present. I don't like the present because the person I am today isn't the person I used to be, and I liked being that person a whole lot better!'

It's an important point, and to answer it, we have to move on to considering the fundamental issues of your old Self, your new Self, and indeed what we even mean by 'Self'.

Key points

- The mind wanders: to the past, the future and other places in the present.
- It's OK if you're choosing to let your mind wander, but a mind wandering of its own accord is often an unhappy mind, especially when something like an LTC gives plenty to worry about.
- A wandering mind makes you more likely to get lost in unhelpful thoughts and feelings.
- When your mind wanders, you can miss out on what's actually happening in the here and now.
- The alternative is present moment awareness, or mindfulness.
- Mindfulness allows you to take part in the world that's going on around you, to enjoy the good parts and face up to the bad parts.
- Mindfulness allows you to treat the present as a secure base and stable anchor for thinking constructively about the future and past.
- You can learn to be more mindful in several ways: through approaching everyday activities differently, through learning formal daily mindfulness practices or by exploring other practices such as yoga or tai chi.

6

Who am I now? A sense of Self

Another weekend brings another argument between Desmond and his daughter Mary. This time, they're discussing the wedding of his granddaughter Lauren in a few weeks' time. Desmond and Lauren have always been close, and he's pleased to see her finally getting married to that young man she's been living with these last few years, especially now they've a baby on the way.

The problem is that the wedding ceremony, the photographs and the reception will involve a lot of walking and standing around, and it's clear to both Desmond and Mary that he's not going to be able to manage all of that.

Desmond's solution is to say he won't go at all, because he doesn't want Lauren's big day to be spoiled by a wheezing old invalid slowing everything down.

Mary's solution is that he should use that nice fold-up wheelchair that she got for him; that way he can stand and sit normally for the bits that matter to him (the ceremony, the photographs), but between times one of his children or grown-up grandchildren can push him around.

And that's where the argument starts, because Desmond's reaction is an absolute 'no'. He says, 'I might not have my health, but I'm not going to be pushed around like a cripple; I'd rather be six feet underground than have people look at me with pity. I've always been a strong, independent man and I'm not going to have people see me like that.'

Although Desmond expresses himself bluntly (as you might expect from an old sailor), his reaction to the idea of using a wheelchair is not uncommon, and though resistance to using a wheelchair is well known,[57] people are reluctant to accept many other things that might actually help – medication, a walking stick, an adapted bed or bathroom. There can, of course, be many different things going on behind this, but one of the commonest – as in Desmond's case – is that this new thing doesn't feel to the person in question as if it fits them – other people may need them, and benefit from them, but I'm not one of those people.

And because it will really matter if Desmond misses his granddaughter's wedding, it's worth us spending some time on just how this sense of 'Self' comes to get in the way so badly, and look at some other ways of approaching it that may prove more useful.

6.1 How your Self can get in the way

This is what Desmond experiences: he has a particular view of what is and isn't OK for the kind of man he is. Now, we might well disagree – possibly strongly – with his perception of what it means for someone to be a wheelchair user; I dare say a large number of people including Paralympian athletes would want to take issue with the idea that they are objects of pity and reduced to 'being pushed around like a cripple', in his words. And anyone trying to help Desmond reconsider his decision might want to challenge some of that.

However, even if he modified these views, there's a strong possibility he wouldn't be much more accepting of the wheelchair for himself. Working with people who are adapting to change in their lives, time and again I have conversations like the following:

MRS SMITH: 'I know the stressed and panicky feelings come from all the stuff that's happened to me – the illness, the treatment – but I still shouldn't be pathetic enough to get into such a state.'

ME: 'If you met someone else, and heard she'd been through all the same things as you, and now she was feeling stressed, would you say she was "pathetic" for being like this?'

MRS SMITH: 'Of course not … I'd say it was fair enough.'

ME: 'So can you say "it's fair enough" that you get stressed by what's happened?'

MRS SMITH: 'But it's different; I can be all understanding for them, but *I* shouldn't be like that!'

Changing an attitude to the situation (whether that's panic or wheelchair use) is not enough in these situations, because a fixed and rigid sense of Self – who I am – gets in the way; maybe it's OK for other people to use a wheelchair, or have panic attacks, only eat soft food or whatever other limitation or adaptation applies, but that's just not *me*.

Experiencing the difference between how you see things are and how (you believe) they ought to be – sometimes called 'dissonance' – has been at the heart of many approaches to psychology, from Freud onwards.[58,59,60] Broadly, a big difference between the two (lots of dissonance) seems to be uncomfortable and will often lead to action to close the gap. So, where reality is worse than how you think things ought to be – for example, you're less fit than you believe you should be – you may be motivated to bring reality 'into line' with your expectation, in this case by exercising. Except, as the many of us who struggle with this know, it isn't always quite that easy; other things get between the intention and the action (e.g. lack of time, lack of opportunity, laziness, lack of persistence).

Sometimes, though, we just can't bring the reality into line with our expectation, because the expectation is unrealistic; so our expectation to become as fit as an athlete is no longer possible even with the best motivation in the world, because some limiting factor exists – such as an LTC that affects muscle or leaves energy levels severely impaired. The risk is that you are then stuck between your idea of what ought to happen and what is actually possible – always disappointed, always frustrated.

The other logical answer to prevent this frustration, though, is not to alter a reality that cannot be altered, but, as the Stoic philosopher Seneca taught, to adjust our expectations;[61] basically develop a more realistic view of how things are, so the gap between expectation and reality isn't so huge.

Seneca was largely talking about our expectation of others and of the world; however, that same principle operates with expectations of ourselves. Maybe sometimes it's not our expectations of the world that need changing, but our expectations of ourselves. Maybe we've always been unrealistic about our ability to be a great athlete, a great singer or someone who is entitled to be completely happy all the time.

Or maybe we have changed, but our idea of ourselves hasn't, so what was once a reasonable expectation isn't any longer. In Desmond's case, above, a few years ago he could easily have been on his feet all day – that was a reasonable expectation of the 'old' Desmond, but not now. And if he compares himself now with himself then, he's likely always to fall short.

So two of the main ways that my ideas about myself can get in the way are a fixed image of who I am that doesn't match reality and (sometimes causing that) a tendency to hold on to who I *used* to be, even though things have changed. The rest of this chapter will discuss ways of trying to deal with these problems.

6.2 Old Self, new Self

'I'm just not the person I used to be.' This is one of the commonest things I hear from people trying to adjust to illness, disability or simply aging. And of course, in one sense it's true; many of the attributes the 21-year-old you had are not there in the 51-year-old you – you may not have the same energy, shape, stamina or fitness. Your visual and mental acuity might be a little less sharp, your hair may be a different colour (or gone), you may be less optimistic, and so on. And there may be positives too – you may have more wisdom, more knowledge, more skills and a wealth of experience of how to deal with challenges that simply weren't there as a youth. It's important to remember those (and other) gains, but they don't mean the losses don't hurt.

Actually, the recognition that you're not the person you were is the battle half-won; because, in our example above, Desmond hasn't fully realised the fact that he has changed and is now exactly the kind of person who makes occasional use of a wheelchair. We'll arrive shortly at the other half of that battle (having realised the change, then accepting it). But first, it's worth taking a few minutes to apply it to yourself.

Exercise 6.1: Old Self/new Self

This exercise should clarify how this changed sense of Self applies in your life. It might turn out to be no great deal at all for you, but I should also warn you that thinking carefully about this stuff can sometimes be quite an emotional business. So make sure you've got enough time to carry on through it, and aren't doing it somewhere you wouldn't want to get upset (on the train, at a café). If you do find yourself getting upset, please don't just give up on the exercise, remembering what we said in Chapter 4: that avoiding doing things because they make us feel bad can lead to a narrower life. So resolve to go through with it, even if you do need a few minutes' break/cup of tea to settle yourself back to it. We will get to a different way of looking at this issue, but first it needs be confronted.

Take a sheet of paper and divide it into two columns, and head them 'THEN, I was ...' and 'NOW, I am ...' as in Figure 6.1 (or use Figure A1.11 in Appendix 1).

THEN, I was ...	NOW, I am ...

Figure 6.1 Aspects of yourself in the past and in the present from Exercise 6.1

For the 'THEN' column, add qualities that defined you at some point in the past – that could be pre-illness, or in your hey-day (whenever you see that as being). Make the list as long as you like, but try for at least eight or ten items. Those items could be psychological (e.g. 'THEN, I was ... confident') or physical (e.g. 'THEN, I was ... able to walk for miles'), social (e.g 'THEN, I was ... in a successful relationship'), or indeed of any other type that seems relevant to you. It might be useful if there were some items you consider negative alongside those you consider positive (e.g. 'THEN, I was ... socially awkward'), but only if you can think of some.

And next, do the same for the 'NOW, I am ...' column. The same rules apply; you may find yourself mainly putting in ones that 'match' the items from the first column (e.g. 'THEN, I was ... confident', 'NOW, I am ... shy and anxious in public'), but there might also be aspects that don't have any equivalent in the 'THEN, I was ...' column. Some (many?) may, of course, have stayed the same, and it might be good to see if there any positive ones alongside the negative.

So for Alina, the young woman with chronic pain problems we have been following, the results might look something like this:

THEN, I was ...	**NOW, I am ...**
Slim	Fatter
Attractive	Unattractive
Sociable	A loner
Fit	Unhealthy
Able to work long hours	Unable to work long hours
Building a good career	Going nowhere
Intelligent	Still intelligent, though not using it
... and so on	... and so on

Figure 6.2 Aspects of Self in the past and in the present – example

So, what do you do with your list? Take a close look at it, especially noticing the following.

- I imagine the 'NOW' list is more negative than the 'THEN' list. If the changes your condition has brought have all been positive, I very much doubt you'd be reading this book! At the same time, though, if there's only positive things about your old Self, and only negative things about your current Self, it may be that there's a distortion creeping into your view; sometimes when our situation is genuinely worse than it used to be, we recall the past as even more entirely wonderful than we would have said at the time – a kind of 'halo' effect. Nostalgia can be pleasant, of course, but in this context it can be quite dangerous; an idealised past can be toxic in at least two ways – it can give an unrealistic target for what you are capable of at your very best, and it will make the present seem even harder to bear because you're comparing it to an exaggerated ideal past.
- How accurate are the negatives? As well as overestimating how good things were in the past, we can underestimate the present. Are there other important positives to the present that aren't listed? Are the negatives too strong or absolute? It's worth trying to check for any obvious distortions; however, you won't be able to reason away all (or maybe any) of them – and that's not what we're trying to do. Rather, just amend any that seem 'over the top' once you look at them again.
- Of the negative things in the 'NOW' column, how many are you genuinely stuck with? For example, Alina might truly be less fit and less able to work long hours than before. However, being 'less sociable' is a way she's choosing to behave rather than something dictated by her condition. That bit can change; it might not be easy, but it can change. We'll look at that more in the next two chapters.
- Accept the present, mourn the past. If you think that the contents of the NOW column do indeed accurately represent you now, take a good look at them. It may not be comfortable, but it is better to get used to the new reality than to carry on assuming that you're 'really' the person in the THEN column – many years ago or before the condition. When I use the word

'accept' here, I'm not meaning you have to be pleased about it, or that you have to give up on improving aspects that can be changed (e.g. Alina could make a concerted attempt to lose some weight). Rather, as we saw in Chapter 4, I'm advising accepting that 'this is the way things are at this moment'. That equally means accepting that things have changed from how they were before (in the THEN column of the exercise). That's no small task, because there may be aspects of 'I, THEN' that you really liked and you really miss. So, it's understandable that you mourn that version of yourself; and I think 'mourning' is the right word, because that's what we do when we're sad at the passing of something important, even though we accept that it has really gone.

The way I explain this to anyone familiar with computer software is that we are talking about 'versions'. Most long-lasting computer programs (and I mean word-processors and spreadsheets rather than many games) keep changing subtly – known bugs are fixed, new features are added. To help keep track of how up-to-date your copy of the program is, the developers will 'number' them. So, initially, your word-processor or spreadsheet may be Version 1.0, but with updates it will become Version 1.1, Version 1.2 and so on. At some point, however, there may be a more major re-design; it will still be the same program at heart, but the changes will be great enough for it to be called Version 2.0. And then, as its own bugs get fixed and newer features are added, that becomes Version 2.1, Version 2.2 and so on.

The reason for discussing this is that it fits some aspect of how we change ourselves; we are constantly changing a little at a time (e.g. Version 1.5 to Version 1.6). But sometimes a much more major change comes along that is more like moving from Version 1.7 to Version 2.0. It's still the same program – the spreadsheet hasn't become a database, 'Microsoft Word' hasn't become 'Adobe Acrobat' – but things have moved on significantly, and they are unlikely to stop moving on as there will be a Version 2.1, 2.2 and so on.

This way of looking at it allows you to acknowledge the continuity of yourself, the constant change, but at the same time acknowledge the significance of some shifts. And though you may remember Version 1.7 with more fondness than Version 2.0, thinking of them this way helps to reinforce the difference between 'I, NOW' and 'I, THEN'.

Having become clearer about the differences between 'I, NOW' and 'I, THEN', and acknowledged that we understandably preferred Version 1.7 to Version 2.0 and will not (and should not) forget our old Self, the important thing to watch out for is the tendency to make comparisons.

> Still on holiday, Bill is cooking a barbecue for his family on a pleasant evening. Clumsily, he knocks into one of the supporting legs of the barbecue and it begins to tip over. Unable to touch the hot top surface, he tries to stop it by grabbing at one of the legs, but doesn't now have the strength of grip in his hands to hold on, and all the cooking food slides off on to the ground. Though his family see the funny side, he is furious with himself, thinking 'Before the MS, I'd easily have stopped that', and he spends the rest of the evening in a far worse mood than a few spoiled sausages merit.

> Caroline, however, has had a good day. She's had barely any time for her voluntary work at the local day centre since Geoff's accident. However, they were so desperate for help for their summer fund-raising fair that she agreed to organise the refreshment stall. And though having Geoff next to her was often more of a hindrance than a help, she manages it well despite business being brisk and several minor problems needing to be sorted out. She is thanked effusively by the organising committee, but when talking to her sister on the phone, she is dismissive of what she has done: 'Yes, it all went pretty smoothly, and I know I haven't done anything like it for a while, but honestly – before all this, I'd have been running the whole event, and a lot more professionally than this lot managed. Don't you see, the fact that it seems like a big achievement to sell a few teas and cakes show just how far I've fallen.'

In each case, the current event, whether bad or good, is not reacted to in its own terms, but instead makes the person compare their current Self with their previous one, and come off worse in the process.

It's as if we get stuck inside a particular 'story' about ourselves, or a set of stories. Desmond has a story about being strong and independent, Alina about being popular and attractive, and Caroline has one about being overburdened and carrying all the responsibility. It's not a question of how accurate these stories are, but simply that, when we define ourselves in terms of them, we become trapped, less able to spot alternative ways of acting. In short, less flexible.

This also illustrates a much wider point: when we get lost in thinking about things, particularly the past, we lose track of what's happening in front of us – it gets harder to make accurate judgements, harder to give things as much or as little credit as they deserve, and harder to get on coping with life. We've already touched on that in our section on present moment awareness (Chapter 5) and defusion (Chapter 4).

6.3 Social Self

It would be a mistake, when considering 'Self' and the problems it brings, only to consider how you make sense of it inside your own head. Because who we are is also greatly affected by others.

Some people, it's true, seem to be pretty much the same whether in a work setting, a private one, alongside a bishop or in a bar. But for many people, their characteristics change with the setting they're in, and particularly with the people around them. One way of looking at this is that some people are just better at matching how they present their 'real' Self to the situation they're in – a trait that is sometimes called 'self-monitoring'.[62] Those who are very aware of how others are around them and alter their own behaviour to fit in are sometimes called 'high self-monitors', while those who tend to act more consistently, irrespective of who is around, are 'low self-monitors'.

But if we think about the person who is different in different settings, which is the 'real' him? If someone is polite but brisk in the office, loud-mouthed and comical in the pub, and short-tempered and controlling in the home, which one is the 'real' him, and which are the masks that he puts on?

Many of us would suspect that there actually isn't any one 'true' Self – that all those traits and mannerisms that make up a person are in part at least a creation of the person's environment, and so every version is equally truly 'them'.

There are certain problems that can crop up because of our social Selves – the version of ourselves that others see. True, some people find it comforting to 'play a role' in times of difficulty, even if they're feeling shaken by a recent diagnosis or unpleasant symptom. The idea of, for example, putting their work clothes on and playing their usual part of office joker or stern boss can be a welcome interruption to worry and doubt.

The difficulties come when the social role we play becomes a limitation on our flexibility – by which I mean that we avoid doing something useful because it's not what others would expect of us, or because we fear their disapproval or pity. That was part of Desmond's reluctance to use a wheelchair at the beginning of this chapter; not only did he not like the idea of being a wheelchair user, he also didn't like the idea of others seeing him as someone who uses one.

One of the main goals in dealing with LTCs is being able to make the right adaptations and changes in order to get the best quality of life under difficult circumstances. Anything that holds us back from spotting a useful change or from putting it into practice is reducing our flexibility, and so reducing our quality of life. Being trapped by our public image is one such limitation on flexibility.

It would be tempting to say that you'd be worrying over nothing in this regard – that no one will bat an eyelid if you suddenly act very differently if that's what's good for you. Well, sometimes that's true, and certainly on the wheelchair issue it's often the case that close friends and family are just pleased to see you out and about rather than a prisoner in your own home. Others, though, will indeed sometimes react in an unhelpful manner.

When one of her oldest friends decided to throw a big party before moving back to the Czech Republic, Alina initially decided not to go; she couldn't face being at a big night out, looking and feeling fat and unable to dance all night like she used to. But that friend, Evka, has been worried about the changes she's seen in Alina, and has been working hard to persuade her to come, out of duty if nothing else.

The evening has arrived and, despite her reluctance and anxiety, Alina is actually having a good time. She's dressed differently than she normally would (to cover up her changed shape as best she can), and she's only allowing herself to get up for one dance in every four or five, rather than being on the dance floor the whole time.

And then one of the young men she used to work the fields with drunkenly tries to drag her up on to the dance floor; when she refuses, he accuses her of being 'boring', and that maybe if she danced more she might lose a few pounds ...

Most of us would be able to sympathise with Alina's horrified response to this; not only has the man been rude to her, but he has voiced the very things she believes and hates about herself. And it's usually those things that hurt us most, rather than things we know to be untrue. No wonder this incident makes Alina believe she should have stuck with her original plan of staying home, and never come out to anything like this again.

Evka finds Alina crying in the toilets, fiddling with her phone to try to arrange for a taxi straight away.

'Come on,' says Evka, 'Greg is just being a drunken jerk, like usual. Since when did any of us take any notice of what he says?'

'He's right, though, isn't he? I *am* fat and I *am* boring and I should never have come here.'

Evka isn't quite sure how to reassure her friend, but (bolstered by the drinks she's already had) decides to be bold.

'Listen, Alina; you came here for a reason tonight. You did it because you wanted to be a good friend to me. And I think you did it because, despite your illness, you'd still like to be around people, enjoying the atmosphere. I'm really sorry Greg upset you, but seriously, if you run home and hide under the duvet every time something about this illness upsets you, then you're in for a lonely time. At times we've all got to put up with feeling bad if we're going to do any of the things that matter to us. So maybe we start by heading back out there and getting on with my party; after we've re-done your eye make-up, anyway; honestly, it makes you look like a depressed panda.'

It's unlikely that Evka's Bacardi-fuelled pep-talk is going to make Alina suddenly accept all the suffering in her life with complete tranquillity, and never have another tear or moment's regret about her pain. However, the essence of what she says – that our lives are impoverished if we give up those things that matter to us in order to avoid discomfort – is at the heart of this book's message, and we'll look at it further in the coming chapters.

So we've seen that the expectations of others can – if we let them – be a limit on our ability to use a new tool (e.g. wheelchair) or coping strategy (e.g. pacing yourself on a night out), and how that can lead us to deny ourselves things that matter. That doesn't make it easy to accept the shame, or the resentment, the anxiety or whatever other unwanted experience is brought about by doing the thing that's right for you, rather than what others expect (or that you want them to see). You'll need to look back at Chapter 4 to remind yourself of some of the ways to cope better with, or indeed accept, the presence of these feelings.

Before we move on from 'social Self', there is another important aspect of the relationship between 'who I am' and other people, and that is …

6.4 Self-as-burden

One of the hardest aspects of Geoff's brain injury for Caroline to deal with is his lack of insight; he doesn't notice, or he forgets, what he cannot now do. He'll commence an ambitious DIY project, only for it to descend into chaos within the first few hours. Or he'll make complex arrangements for meeting relatives in town, and genuinely believe that he'll remember the details, so doesn't bother writing them down; inevitably, within minutes he will have forgotten everything.

And yet Caroline will sometimes be taken by surprise by his understanding.

One evening, Caroline slumps into her chair with a sigh, and is telling Geoff about the long list of things she's had to do that day, and how tired she now is, when she notices that he's started to cry, something she's almost never seen him do.

It takes some coaxing to get him to say what's upset, him; but eventually he says:

'You're so tired all time, and you get ill; you're running around looking after me, or doing stuff I should be doing for you. You should just be doing things you want to: looking after the grandchildren, doing your voluntary work. Instead, you're so sad and worn down; and I'm doing that to you. You'd be so much better off without me – I'm just a burden.'

Working as I do with people with cancer, degenerative conditions or severely limiting LTCs, I hear variations of this all the time. And I know my colleagues who are nurses, doctors and care assistants do as well. Speaking personally, it always hurts a little to hear it, because it's usually so deeply meant and deeply felt. It's often at its strongest in relation to partners and close family, because, in loving them, we mostly want to make their lives more full of happiness, rather than filled with fatigue, worry and restrictions that being a carer can bring. And I think that's often especially true when the ill person was previously a main care-giver; like a mother who saw her role as enabling her children to flourish and live an independent life, and now sees these grown-up children putting aspects of their own lives 'on hold' to care for her.

Within the tremendously controversial area of requests for euthanasia, one aspect that concerns many professionals in my field is the motivation (sometimes well hidden) to die quickly not because of personal physical or emotional suffering, but rather to relieve the perceived burden of care for partners and children.

How can we respond to someone feeling this acute sense of being a burden? It's natural, but I'd say unhelpful, for the partner to blatantly lie and claim that there *is* no extra work, that any increased responsibility for childcare, housework, bread-winning or transport is not tiring, that disrupted sleep from helping their partner with night-time medical routines has no effect. To a greater or lesser extent, these things do have an impact, and as the condition is long term, so generally is the impact.

If we accept the reality that there is indeed a 'burden' on the care-giver, the important thing is to be ruthlessly clear about exactly what that burden is:

The illness is the burden, not the person who has it.

So, in Caroline's case, it is the brain injury that is the burden, *not* Geoff himself, who doesn't choose to have these needs. That might sound as if I'm splitting hairs, but, if so, then it's a really important hair to split, because buying into that unhelpful and inaccurate belief that you personally are the burden actually just increases the sum total of suffering going on; neither you nor your carer/partner benefits from adding guilt, self-loathing and depression to the problems that already exist.

Many people have reached the same conclusion about the importance of recognising the difference between 'the person' and 'the illness'; we would rightly be upset these days if a doctor were to refer to someone you loved as 'the case of Parkinson's Disease in Bed 12' (and thankfully that seems a lot less common than it used to be). But just as we shouldn't tolerate others regarding us just as our illness, we shouldn't fall into doing it ourselves. The simple fact is that you are the person who has that condition (alongside a million other attributes); you are not that condition.

And we can go further in thinking about this. When talking to a couple where the question of 'being a burden' has come up, I'll often discuss the idea that the illness is the burden, not the person, because the person didn't choose this. And, instead, I ask the couple to consider that an illness comes into that couple's life, and affects both of them in different ways. It is as if it reaches into one person and causes pain, or reduced mobility, fatigue or whatever the relevant physical symptoms are, *and* it reaches into their partner and creates tiredness, and worry, and too-many-things-to-do, and so on. In doing so, I encourage them to see the condition as an almost 'external' thing, with tendrils reaching into each of them creating these effects.

This is mainly to reinforce the separation of 'condition' and 'person' to undermine the sense of self-as-burden. Though, to reiterate what was said in Chapter 3, remember that you can never really prevent a thought from occurring or successfully eliminate it; recognising that you don't buy into it helps you retain some distance and reduces the extent to which you see the world through its eyes.

There's a second reason for putting forward that image of the illness as a separate thing reaching into all the family members: it can help couples visualise the problem as something they can face together. To go back to the title of this book, they can face that as the enemy, rather than feeling like it's a battle between them.

Incidentally, the importance of not seeing our selves in terms of particular attributes (that we aren't too fond of) certainly isn't new. A well-respected American psycho-therapist called Irvin Yalom wrote about one of his patients, a man with advanced cancer, who one day realised that he was more than just his worst attributes; he said he had been in a meeting, staring down at his feet, when it struck him that just because his shoes were shabby didn't make him a shabby person – he was much more than that one aspect of himself. His phrase 'I am not my shoes' became a shorthand for not judging oneself by one attribute.[63]

And, finally, this perspective on 'who I am' as being separate from 'the condition I have' or 'things that have happened to me' can point towards a different way of looking at what the 'Self' is.

6.5 What does 'Self' mean?

I can appreciate that this may sound like an abstract and rather philosophical question to ask, but I think it's directly relevant to coping with an LTC – or indeed life in general.

Why? Because in this chapter we've seen several examples of how your view of yourself can cause problems – Desmond did miss his much-loved granddaughter's wedding because of it, Bill spent part of his family holiday furious with himself because of it, Alina almost gave up entirely on socialising and Caroline's husband decided he was ruining her life because of how he saw himself. If the 'Self' brings such problems, it must be worth looking at what it actually is.

6.5.1 The Observing Self

To start with, let's return to a question that may have struck you when we were looking at 'versions' of the Self, in section 6.2 above. The emphasis was upon recognising and coming to accept the changes in ourselves that time inevitably brings, and especially if illness or other adversity comes along.

But if there's so much change in the Self, what exactly is there that stays the same? Or, to put it another way, just how much change can you experience and still be 'you'? Are we just like the broom someone claims to have had for 40 years, even though they've replaced the handle twice and the head three times? The analogy isn't too far-fetched, because the overwhelming majority of cells in any of our bodies are dying and being replaced all the time.

From the ACT approach (and similar ideas have been long held elsewhere), there is one sense of the 'Self' that is continuous, no matter what changes happen to a person: that which observes those changes. When you practised defusing from thoughts in Chapter 3, there was a part of your mind that was noticing the thoughts, separate from the thoughts themselves. Similarly, in noticing unwanted feelings in Chapter 4. And the same observing part of the mind was in the 'staying present' exercises in Chapter 5, noticing when the mind wandered and gently bringing it back to the here and now.

Sometimes, that's referred to as the **Observing Self**, and it's the part that stays the same while everything else changes – it's the common element in the me of 30 years ago starting at university and the me of today; two quite different versions of me with different experiences, knowledge, assumptions, physical attributes, scars both physical and emotional, family and so on and so on and so on.

Being clear about the separation of this pure, Observing Self can help us step back from the melee of thoughts, feelings, symptoms and events we experience from moment to moment.

And if you just leave it at that – recognising there's an Observing Self that can ride the storm of moment-to-moment experience, no matter how turbulent it is – then you will be able to avoid many of the problems we've discussed in this chapter.

However, we can take that thinking a little further. It's a relatively new approach[64] that can seem a little more complex at first, but it opens up new possibilities for making sense of and then dealing with our experiences. Please feel free to skip to the end of the chapter if you prefer, but if you're interested, read on.

6.5.2 Flexible perspective-taking

Recognising the Observing Self is useful. And we can then start considering in more detail what is being observed and how; which brings us to the act of 'perspective-taking'.

If we talk of an artist taking a perspective in painting something (a landscape, maybe), then we'd mean that they were looking *at* a particular thing (a mountain) *from* a particular place (a valley); and, if we think about it, we should add *at* a particular moment (twilight). Changes to any of those elements of the perspective would lead to a different painting; for instance, Claude Monet painted many images of

London's Houses of Parliament from across the Thames; they varied in time of day, with resultant variations of weather, and are remarkable viewed side by side[65] (easily done online, impossible in any one gallery).

So perspective-taking means observing something from a particular place at a particular time. Arguably the most important perspective we take in our own lives is of I, HERE, NOW; I've been introducing those words (complete with capitals) gradually over the last few chapters. To look at them in more detail:

- **I** (as distinct from YOU/HIM/HER/IT/THEM): it is the thoughts, feelings, sensations and experiences that are happening in me, and to me, which I'm observing. Not the thoughts, feelings or experiences of someone else.
- **HERE** (as distinct from THERE): the observation is of what is happening in me, to me and around me in this situation – not what is happening elsewhere or what might happen if things were different.
- **NOW** (as distinct from THEN): the things happening right now, rather than last week, last year or next year.

Many elements of this I, HERE, NOW stance have cropped up before in this book; in Chapter 3 we've practised recognising that thoughts are not realities, but are things happening inside us which we can step back from, observe and not get tangled up in (defuse from). In Chapter 5 we practised recognising and returning to the here and now, rather than losing track and getting caught up in other places and other times.

It's important to understand, though, that being I, HERE, NOW is not everything, and is not the only stance we want to take. You may want to reflect on and learn from what you experienced last time pain and fatigue stopped you from going on an evening out: you would then be taking the perspective of I, HERE, THEN.

Equally, we may want to think about what we would do if we were currently in a different situation – for example, I might wonder if I would be better off if I was doing this job in central London rather than rural Herefordshire? My perspective at that moment would be I, THERE, NOW (and I being the person I am, the answer would definitely be 'no'!).

Or I might be talking to a colleague at work and trying to understand why she seems irritated by what I am saying, in which case I'd be using YOU, HERE, NOW.

Why do we emphasise these particular components (I, HERE, NOW)? For several reasons:

- We've already seen that it's important to be able to stay in the HERE and NOW rather than allowing your mind to be dragged off into future, past or elsewhere
- It looks as if one of the basic ways that children learn to make sense of how they relate to all the other things and people in their world is by learning to tell the difference between I and YOU (or HIM, HER or IT), between HERE and THERE, and between NOW and THEN.[66] These continue to be at the core of how we approach the world.
- Being able to put yourself in another's shoes (e.g. YOU, THERE, THEN) allows you to make better sense of their actions and responses. It increases your ability to appreciate their emotional reactions ('empathy') and allows you to recognise how others may have a different view of the situation – in psychology, this is often termed 'Theory of Mind'[67] and is the foundation of social living.
- It helps us to recognise that things change (from THEN to NOW) and distance ourselves from fixed ideas of how things 'always' are for us, or how we should 'always' be.

To apply this back to coping with LTCs, I pointed out earlier how different aspects of 'Self' caused problems for each of the people we've been following. Let's look at that again, using this 'perspective-taking' view of what the Self means:

- Desmond missed his much-loved granddaughter's wedding because he couldn't accept being someone who needed to use a wheelchair. He was seeing himself in terms of I, HERE, THEN rather than I, HERE, NOW; he is still him – the Self observing what is going on is I – but the NOW component has changed with his deteriorating health. Seeing the NOW version of himself as someone willing to use a tool (a wheelchair) for an important job (attending the wedding) might not be easy, but will allow him to make more of his life.

- Much the same is true for Bill, angry with himself for lacking the strength to stop a barbecue toppling over. Expecting himself to have that strength is part of I, HERE, THEN thinking rather than I, HERE, NOW; recognising that change and being able to take the new perspective may help him accept the change – even if there is still regret at the difference.
- Caroline's husband Geoff became distraught at the idea of being a burden to her. We've already discussed a different way of looking at that – namely that the condition is the burden, not the person. Caroline herself, however, was able to make a shift in perspective during this conversation, from seeing things purely from the I, HERE, NOW position to the YOU, HERE, NOW position – seeing the situation through Geoff's eyes. And Caroline being the person she is, she'll be far more careful about taking account of Geoff's reaction to what she says, no matter how overwhelmed with responsibility she feels herself.

But can we get any better at recognising these perspectives, and taking others? I'd say yes.

Exercise 6.2: Flexible perspective-taking

Watch some TV (rare that a psychology book will advise that ...), looking out for some sort of drama (maybe soap opera) where you have the chance to learn something about the characters. A 'fly-on-the-wall' documentary might also be good. Look out for a scene involving at least two people in conversation.

Now try to see that situation from the point of view of one of the participants. What do they seem to think about the situation? How do they feel emotionally? How might they feel physically during that scene?

Now switch to the other character's perspective. What are they feeling? What do they think? Why do they see it that way? If you know enough about the character's 'back-story', how might they have felt differently if they'd been in this situation five years ago?

Note that you can't know for sure what they'd be thinking or feeling; the aim here isn't to be 'right' about their perspective, but simply to try to see the world through another's eyes.

And now put yourself into that scene. If you were involved, what might you be thinking about the matter in hand? How would you be feeling? What would you think of doing? What if a younger version of you was in that scene?

Then, at some point, do the same thing when you're in a real social situation. Try working out in your head the perspective of one of the other people you're with: literally first, what are they seeing from their chair that's different to what you see from yours? What might they be thinking? Feeling?

When you're doing this exercise, it's important to remember that you're not likely to be completely accurate in these other perspectives – either how you would have seen things at a different place or time, or how another person sees or saw them. For our purposes, it is simply the act of purposefully shifting perspective – practising flexible perspective-taking – that brings benefits, both when used in exercises like this and as a habit to get into.

And what are those benefits?

- It makes **defusion** easier; it becomes obvious that the assumptions and thoughts our minds are telling us now would probably look different to a different person, in a different setting, or at a different time. And therefore, it's harder to get trapped into the fused position that these thoughts are realities.

    When Bill knocked over the barbecue, his mind told him that this was because he was less of a man than before and had become pitiful. If he had seen it through his wife's eyes or his children's, he would have realised that other views were equally possible (e.g. that it was just a funny thing that happened, without larger significance).

• It makes it easier to avoid getting stuck inside a story about yourself. We saw earlier in this chapter how a fixed view of 'what I am' can become a cage, and make it harder to deal with what is actually happening around you. This particular form of fusion can be especially limiting, and is weakened by the ability to take more than one perspective on a situation.

> Caroline has agreed to give up a day of other activities to look after her poorly grandson Alfie; a heavy cold means he can't go into day-care, but his mum can't afford a day off work. At one point in the afternoon, she catches her mind drifting back into her old story about 'Everybody puts on me – I never get to do anything for myself'. And then she remembers what she's been taught about switching perspective, and sees the room through little Alfie's eyes – feeling snuffly and a bit miserable, but with his grandma making him drinks and reading him stories. Then her 'put upon' story just doesn't seem to matter any more.

• It makes **acceptance** of unwanted feelings easier. When we experience emotional or physical discomfort, and struggling against it will only make things worse, then a wider perspective can help. We could shift time perspective from NOW to THEN (in the future) and recognise – in the ancient phrase – 'this, too, shall pass'. The suffering is what it is in this moment, and it will be different in the future. Or widening the perspective from I, HERE can help with the recognition that there is more in our world than this suffering – a point we'll return to in the next chapter.

> At times when Alina has to take a break at work to rest her feet, she resents both the pain and the frustration of having to stop when others keep going. Sometimes, though, she pictures the whole hotel busily whirring

away. She pictures herself as part of that bigger picture, responsible for her parts of it running smoothly, and 'fast forwards' in her mind's eye to the point in a few minutes' time when she will be part of the whirring herself again. It helps her put up with the enforced rest.

• It makes acceptance of change easier. Seeing the 'bigger picture' can help counteract the tendency to struggle against those changes that we can't do anything about.

  Sometimes, when Desmond finds himself missing the life at sea and regretting how little he contributes to the world these days, he looks through some of the naval history books that family members always seem to give him for birthday or Christmas gifts. Seeing those World War II sailors, who followed the World War I ones, back to Nelson's navy during the Napoleonic Wars makes him feel part of a continuous story. The fact that newer generations are carrying on, and will hand to others in turn, makes it feel less unfair that his time at sea came to an end.

• It helps when handling difficult situations such as negotiations and conflict. This isn't a recipe for just being so 'understanding' that you always give in. Whether you are genuinely interested in meeting the other person's needs while reaching a 'win–win' outcome, or simply wanting to undermine their arguments and position effectively, it's always useful to be able put yourself in their position (take their perspective: YOU, HERE, NOW) and see what's driving their behaviour in this situation.

There is one major facet of the Self – of what makes you who you are – that we haven't examined in this chapter; that is your Values. It is such an important element of the ACT approach that it will be central to the rest of the book.

Key points

- Your sense of Self can get in the way of living your life, by cutting down which options you're willing to consider, and making you less likely to accept when things have changed.
- By facing, in detail, the changes that life and LTCs bring, you can cope better with them, even if it is uncomfortable to do so.
- We change constantly, sometimes in small amounts, occasionally by a big step; we never truly stay the same for long.
- Accept the present, mourn the past.
- You can get stuck in a 'story' about yourself – a rigid set of ideas about who you are that will limit your flexibility.
- You can also get caged in by an image of yourself that you portray to others, and how you want to be perceived.
- One of the most distressing reactions to having an LTC is if you believe you are a burden to others; it is vital to remember that the *condition* is the burden, not *you*.
- Just as you are not your illness, neither are you your thoughts or your feelings; the underlying 'Self' is the Observing Self – the part of you that notices all those other things happening inside you.
- The Observing Self can take many different perspectives; although I, HERE, NOW is your steady base and anchor, being able to consider the perspective of other people, other places and other times can aid defusion, acceptance and dealing with others.

Living with purpose
Finding your Values

7.1 Aims

> Since Alina's friend Evka returned to the Czech Republic,
> the two have kept in touch. Their video chats matter a
> great deal to both of them, but especially to Alina who
> sees few others. One night she is particularly low, and
> complains:
> 'I'm going nowhere, Evka. All the things I was aiming
> for have been taken away by this illness; I wanted a great
> career, but I'm off sick as much as I'm in these days – I'll
> be lucky to keep my job, let alone get promoted. I was
> beginning to get back into running, thought I'd maybe
> work up to a marathon, but that's all off now. And I
> thought it wouldn't be long before I met someone nice –
> you know, settle down, marry, kids in a few years … Even
> if I went out enough to meet anyone, who'd want me fat
> and useless? Sometimes, I wonder – what's the point?'

7.1.1 Aims and goals

Here's one of the big problems that an LTC can bring; as well
as getting in the way of some of the things you do, it can get
in the way of the things you were *going* to do. Of course, some
of the things Alina mentions will still be possible for her – as
we've already seen, she can certainly socialise, so long as she
accepts some limitations. She could also do something about

her weight, though it might not be easy. However, as for many people with LTCs, some plans may simply not be realistic any more – I daresay there have been people who have trained for and run marathons with fibromyalgia, but they'll be rare. If you develop epilepsy, you're not going to be an airline pilot. Parkinson's Disease with tremor in the hands rules out being a neurosurgeon.

To most of us, those things were never aims anyway; however, we will have had some aim or ambition at some points in our lives. When I was eight or so, most of the boys I knew were destined either to be an astronaut or to lift the World Cup for England. Or both. Fortunately, neither is my goal now, because ambitions change as time passes. Age and maturity will be one source of change; events and learning will prompt others. And changes in health and fitness will alter some of them.

It's worth spending a little time reflecting on the goals we have had. As ever, I'm not expecting anyone's recall to be perfect (or indeed unbiased, though that's another story).[68] Just try this exercise:

Exercise 7.1: Aims in life

Think back to the following stages in your life. At each point, what do you remember being your aims? Perhaps you didn't think much about such things at that point, so maybe imagine going back and talking to that younger version of you, and saying 'What do you want to be in the future? What are your ambitions? What are you working towards?'

It might be worth writing down your answers; there's a form in Appendix 1 (see Figure A1.12).

1 *Earliest aims.* As a young child – can you recall what you wanted to be when you grew up?
2 *Entering adulthood (aged 16/18/21).* Whatever age you feel you were becoming more of an adult than a child – what were your aims then? Not so much idle fantasies as real ambitions; lots of people might fantasise about being a major film star, but only

include it if that was your definite focus – for example, you were trying to get into drama school, making low-budget movies with friends and so on. If someone asked you back then, 'Where do you hope to be in your life by the time you're 30, or 40 or 50?', what might the answer have been?

3 *More recently, before illness started to affect your outlook/abilities.* This one only really applies if you're reading this book as someone whose life has been affected by an LTC – whether your own or that of someone close to you. Before that condition came into your life (that can be either at the point symptoms started, or when you got a diagnosis, or when the symptoms began to intrude more), what were your aims and ambitions – what were you hoping for, what did you think you might reasonably achieve?

4 *Now.* With things exactly as they are in your life right now, what are your goals and ambitions? Again, as far as possible leave aside 'Well, if I won the lottery tomorrow …' answers, and instead focus on the things you genuinely want to achieve; and that might include keeping hold of things you already have (e.g. a successful relationship) as well as gaining new ones.

And now, looking back over all those answers, what do you notice? For most people, they change. Even leaving aside the youngest 'I want to be an astronaut' stage, there is likely to be some degree of change between young adult, older but pre-health problem and today.

Try to work out *why* they changed – was it due to changing preferences (e.g. from wanting a life of travel and adventure to stability and family life), or changed opportunities, or becoming aware of limitations you didn't previously realise?

7.1.2. Letting go of goals

Many times, these major life goals just change gradually without our noticing; sometimes they change all of a sudden and very obviously. There's a scene in the movie *Little Miss*

Sunshine where a teenage character who has been utterly fixated on becoming a jet pilot discovers he's colour-blind and realises in that instant that his goal is now impossible. Understandably, his reaction is extreme. Being forced to let go of a highly prized goal is hugely painful, as anyone who has spent time around young sports participants or seen losing contestants on talent shows will be aware.

I would hope that, this far into the book, you won't be surprised to hear me say that there's no way of preventing or avoiding the experience of pain when you find yourself in that situation; acceptance that the pain is present, not doing things to escalate the problem – those principles from Chapter 4 are the best path to take if it really is the moment to let go of a cherished goal.

It may well be painful to let go of an ambition when it is time to do so; there are far more problems lurking, though, if you either let go of your goals too soon or hang on to them too long.

Back in the early 1990s, I was working with a lot of young men who were living with HIV, at a time when life-extending drugs were only just coming into use. Many of them, upon finding out they were HIV-positive, were faced with the prospect of becoming very ill and dying soon. Understandably enough, many gave up on long-term plans and ambitions (e.g. gradually working towards qualifications and a career that they initially planned), and decided to simply 'live for the day'. I was meeting them a couple of years later, when they were still physically well and with no way of knowing how long they had until they started to decline. Many were bored of partying and living for short-term pleasures, but had lost the sense of direction and purpose that they had prior to their illness, because they had felt their aspirations no longer applied. Consequently, they were feeling rather lost and aimless. The phrase I heard them use more than once was 'past my sell-by date'.

And though this state was very noticeable in that group of people, it certainly isn't confined to them; you see it in people with all kinds of serious and long-term health problems, either because they end up doing better than was expected, or sometimes because they have been overly pessimistic early in their condition. But let's remember that the very nature of many of these conditions is uncertain, so it's often impossible to say exactly what *is* a realistic outlook for any one individual.

The opposite of letting go of goals too early is hanging on to them too long. When something is no longer realistic, doggedly and persistently pursuing it can really get in the way of coping well; large amounts of energy, or money or other resources can get used up in the pursuit with no payoff other than frustration at constant failure. The other way it gets in the way is by stopping you from pursuing more appropriate and achievable goals.

Even five years ago, Desmond was struggling with his health; he was getting shorter of breath and was unable to walk long distances. He could still get to the local shop and return carrying a few items, but a whole day out was difficult. Even keeping track of paperwork and organising things was getting difficult – as much as he hated to admit it, age and worsening health were also affecting his concentration.

And that was becoming a major problem, because his main purpose in life at that time was running the HMS Pearl Association – a club of people who had served on that vessel, and particularly those who had been on board the day it sank. He was always at his most fulfilled when writing to old ship-mates, and putting comrades back in touch with each other. With the 50th anniversary coming up, Desmond had been busy organising a reunion and an official service of remembrance.

Unfortunately, it was just too much for him, and he was beginning to make mistakes. Even though he realised that he should hand over more of the organising to others, he was absolutely determined to see the project through and so insisted on carrying on. When things had gone too far, booking deadlines had been missed and the Association's paperwork was in chaos, other members forced him to give it up. He felt ashamed of his failure and took it all to heart.

Of course, he attended the service and the reunion, but he found it hard to talk about his role in it, and once the event was over, he became more and more withdrawn. In fact, his daughter Mary sees that as the point at which her father 'gave up' and started descending into the pit he's in now.

Desmond shows us the 'double-edged sword' of having goals; they can give a person energy and purpose, and can even stave off some of the effects of aging and extend life.[69] However, hang on to them too long, when they're no longer realistically achievable, and they can make everything worse, putting you under stress, increasing your experience of failure and damaging your self-esteem. As we'd say in ACT, carrying on behaving in the same way because it used to work – even though it doesn't now – is just going to increase your suffering.

As in Desmond's case, it's perfectly understandable that people hang on to important goals too long; reasons might include reluctance to accept the reality of how they've changed (sometimes termed 'denial'); or, as in the last chapter, they may be hanging on to a self-image that is no longer applicable.

Or sometimes it may be because those goals are all they have to cling to – if they're taken away or given up, then that person can lose all sense of purpose and worth. That's exactly what Mary saw happening to Desmond.

The obvious solution is to find another goal, something more appropriate to work towards. But that isn't always straightforward.

Over the next few months, Mary tried again and again to find an alternative interest for Desmond. She suggested he got more involved in the church, bought him model boat kits to build, even suggested he should have a cat to look after. He wasn't interested in any of them, and finally told her to stop interfering or he wouldn't allow her through his door. They both knew he didn't really mean that, but, all the same, Mary realised she wasn't making any progress.

The point is that – contrary to what you might sometimes hear – a goal isn't in itself necessarily a good thing; helping the church, finishing a model boat or caring for a cat were all goals, but of no use to Desmond. Goals are only useful and vitality-giving if they *matter* to that individual.

The secret, then, isn't to focus so much on the *goal* but on *what matters* to a person. And another way of saying that is to focus on *what they value*.

7.2 Values

7.2.1 From goals to Values

I've previously written[70] about a man who was devastated that his declining health meant that he wouldn't be able to teach his son to fish, which he had always looked forward to doing. It was perfectly reasonable to feel sad about losing something like that. Even so, he and I were trying to find out what to do about it. In the end, we tried to pin down what were the qualities – the 'essential ingredients' we called them at the time – of teaching his son to fish that made it important to him. We worked out that the main ones were spending time with his son, teaching his son something that might stay with him into adult life (as fishing had done for him since his own father taught him) and creating some lasting memories for his son. Then, without ignoring that it was a real loss not to be able to teach the fishing, we tried to find something else to aim to do instead. It might not be as good as the fishing, but something that would contain those same 'essential ingredients'. They guided us to choosing 'teach my son chess' instead – not his first choice, but still matching the qualities that made 'teaching fishing' matter to him.

That was many years ago. These days I still sometimes work through that sort of problem with some of the people who come to see me; the biggest difference is that rather than talking about 'essential ingredients' that make something important, I use the term favoured in ACT, and talk about **Values.**

7.2.2 *What I mean by Values*

In the English language, the word 'value' can mean many things; in this approach to LTC management – and indeed living in general – we use the word Values in a particular way (and I'll start the word with a capital V just to show when I'm using it in this sense). By Values, I mean what the therapist and writer Russ Harris describes as 'what we want to stand for in life, how we want to behave, what sort of person we want to be, what sort of strengths and qualities we want to develop'.[71]

If that sounds abstract, then here are some examples:

- The 'teach my son to fish' man from before had, as one of his Values, 'being part of my children's lives'.
- Bill has (among others) 'caring for those close to me'.
- Alina has (among others) 'making the most of opportunities'.
- Caroline has (among others) 'being helpful'.
- Desmond has (among others) 'being loyal'.

I come across many different Values in the people I see; here are a few examples:

- 'being loyal'
- 'being dependable'
- 'helping those in need'
- 'being creative'
- 'being curious'
- 'promoting justice/fairness'
- 'appreciating beauty'
- 'getting things done'
- 'respecting traditions'
- 'influencing others'
- 'leading'
- 'experiencing new things'
- 'having excitement'
- 'looking after my health'
- 'being emotionally close to those I love'
- 'living in a spiritual or religious way'
- 'having self-control'
- 'being honest'

- 'looking after those I love'
- 'being in contact with nature'
- 'being respectful towards others'
- 'nurturing others/helping them develop'
- 'being competitive'
- 'making a contribution to the world'
- 'being sociable'
- 'setting myself challenges (because I want to, not because I have to)'
- 'being a good "team-player"'
- 'being fun-loving'.

It's worth remembering a couple of things about a list like that. First, the precise wording doesn't matter too much (words aren't reality!), so there's nothing magical about the exact phrasing of, for example, 'being caring towards those close to me' instead of 'nurturing those I love'. And, second, no such list could be complete; I hear new Values or new variations on them all the time.

7.2.3 Where Values show up in life

When I'm working individually with someone, we often discover Values without going through a list like the one above, because the evidence of your Values is there in things that are important.

If you look at things that you really enjoy doing, or things you make the opportunity to do even if it's not easy to get the chance, then the reason they matter to you probably involves one or more of your Values. And if you ask yourself 'Why is this so important to me?', you may be able to spot them.

One of his colleagues comments that Bill always insists on taking the day of his wife's birthday off work to celebrate with her, even if it is inconvenient for the projects they are working on. Bill has no problem explaining it: 'It's not so much that it's her birthday, it's just that it matters to prioritise the people who're important to you, and so does enjoying doing nice things with them.'

For Bill, 'prioritising people who're important to you' would count as a Value.

And the opposite applies too – things that particularly hurt a person may well show something important about what they Value – because things that don't matter very much usually don't hurt so much. The phrase we often use in ACT is 'Inside your pain, you'll find your Values'.

Desmond has found it very hard to let go of his responsibilities for the HMS Pearl Association; it's been a blow to his pride and made him recognise how much more limited he's become. The hardest moment of all, though, comes a few months later, when he receives a message back from another member after Desmond announced he was stepping down. The message thanks him for all he has done, and the writer goes on to say what a lifeline Desmond's newsletters and personal messages have been; so few people understand what they've been through, and the world seems happy to ignore the 'forgotten conflicts' that went on after World War II. If the HMS Pearl Association folds now (understandably given the age and poor health of the few surviving members), he'll feel that bit more alone.

That really strikes at Desmond: partly because being a part of something has always mattered to him too, but also because it feels as if he's letting his old shipmate down, and he realises that both reliability and loyalty are very important to him.

So, even if he can't run the whole association, he decides that he'll keep writing to at least a few of the members.

Desmond's case shows us a couple of important points: by considering those events or moments that cause us real emotional pain (to use an old-fashioned phrase, that 'pierce you to the heart'), we can learn about the things that really matter to us.

And the second thing we learn from him is this: having realised the Values that were being let down by giving up contact with other colleagues, he was able to choose another action (letter-writing) that would fulfil some of the same needs.

There's a wider point here about Values too: living life according to your Values will bring you more fulfilment, more vitality and more sense of a life well lived. And the other side of that coin is that 'Inside your Values, you'll find your pain'. The very act of Valuing means that when (whether through your own fault or not) a given Value gets neglected, then your life gets narrower and less fulfilling; and when it gets transgressed or contravened, it really hurts. If you Value close loving contact with those you care for, and then you're separated from them for a period, that's going to hurt. Similarly, if you Value striving for excellence, and usually express this through work, then if you have to retire through ill health, you're going to suffer.

Unless, like Desmond – and others we've met – you find a different way of serving that Value. Just like the man who wanted to teach his son to fish and ended up teaching him chess instead, if we know what Values make something important to us, then we can work creatively to 'serve' those Values in a different way, even if (and especially if) circumstances are difficult. If someone Values 'being part of my kids' childhood' but is too ill to play football, then they can read stories, or watch DVDs together and talk about what's going on – they may have preferred to be playing football, but these alternatives still serve the same Value. Similar things can even be done where separation is total; the charity Storybook Dads enables fathers who are in prison to record CDs or DVDs of themselves reading bedtime stories for their children,[72] and sister organisations do the same for imprisoned mothers and for armed forces parents serving overseas.

In the next chapter, we'll look more closely at how these Values can be put into action. For now, I want to clarify a few points about this view of Values – it helps prevent possible confusion.

7.2.4 What Values are and aren't

- *Values are chosen.*
  When I talk of Values, I'm talking about something that you choose, that you want to be about – rather than something

that you're stuck with or feel has been imposed upon you. So, if you think that being polite and respectful to others is really important to you even if others disagree, it's a Value. However, maybe you're polite and respectful to others because your parents/teachers/priest drummed it into you, and you've ended up feeling guilty and bad if you aren't polite, yet inside you want to be irreverent, challenging and cheeky (maybe thinking the world would be a whole lot better if everyone was). Then politeness isn't really one of your Values – it's an expectation of others that you might or might not choose to conform with.

That's not to say that some of your Values aren't traceable back to important figures in your life, or religious teachings, or favourite books; the question is whether you, as an autonomous adult, choose and claim them as your own now, whether or not those sources ever know about it. This approach isn't in opposition to people living by political or religious Values, so long as that person genuinely accepts that Value as how they choose to be on their own behalf. Maybe a time of change and crisis is the moment to check that your Values really are *yours*. The psychotherapist and concentration-camp survivor Viktor Frankl said it clearly: 'Everything can be taken from a man or a woman but one thing: the last of human freedoms – to choose one's attitude in any given set of circumstances, to choose one's own way'.[73]

- *Values don't depend on others' approval.*
  Other people may be aware of these Values (e.g. 'the thing about Desmond is that he takes loyalty very seriously'), but the judgement of others is not what they are about; the question is how you would choose to be even if no one else ever knew. Because while it might be nice to have your qualities noticed and appreciated by others, Desmond would still be loyal even if no one was around to see; Caroline would inconvenience herself massively to keep a commitment and probably never mention the trouble she had gone to. Each of them would be acting that way because it was, to them, the *right* thing to do.

- *Values are not the same as goals.*
  When asked what they Value, some people's first answers may be along the lines of 'owning my own home', 'getting

married', 'living to see my children grow up'. Those may be very important things, but specifically they're important *goals* rather than *Values*. The difference is that goals are achievements or states that may or may not happen – at some point you can say, 'Yes, that's done; I now own my own house/am married/have seen my children grow up and become parents themselves.' And then what? Well, there will be other goals that matter to you, and you may be working towards them too. A Value, though, is something that's never 'done' – it's more of a guiding principle throughout your life, and may well be the reason that those goals matter to you in the first place. Working towards those goals is 'in the service of' those Values.

○ Desmond's goal of keeping in touch with his shipmates is in the service of his Values of 'being loyal' and 'being dependable'.
○ Bill's goal of making a fuss of his wife on her birthday is in the service of his Value of 'treating the people you love as a priority'.
○ Caroline has a goal of getting her husband involved in support organisations for people with a brain injury, just in case she becomes too ill to look after him all the time; that's not driven by any sense of self-preservation, but by her Value of 'protecting those you love'.
○ Alina is aiming one day to be manager of a hotel; this goal is in service of her Value of 'making the most of opportunities'.

One way of looking at the difference between Values and goals is that Values are like compass directions, guiding which way to head (e.g. West), whereas goals are like destinations along that route (e.g. Bristol, Cardiff, Cork, Nova Scotia, Quebec). With the destinations (goals), you can arrive there, and the journey's done. With the direction (Values), you can always carry on travelling West. So, getting your child into a good school may well be an important goal in the service of 'nurturing those you love', but, having achieved it, the Value will continue to exist and you will find yourself serving it in many different ways.

Hopefully, it's clear that goals aren't unimportant (and we'll revisit them in the next chapter), but they are different to Values. And when circumstances require, our goals may need to change, yet the Values being served will still be the same; that's what was going on in the example above of the man who wanted to teach his son to fish (a goal), in the service of 'being involved in my child's life' (a Value), who settled on teaching him chess (a goal), which served the same Value.

That said, Values themselves aren't unchangeable and cast in concrete: some will be constant through life; others will change as our experience unfolds and our circumstances change.

- *Values are not the same as actions.*
  Living according to your Values will require actions, but just as they are not the same as goals, they are not individual actions either; instead, you could think of them as 'types of action', or even 'ways of acting'. If it wasn't so clumsy, we might rephrase them so that 'being caring' became 'acting in a caring manner'. That's why most of them involve words with –ing at the end, such as 'nurturing …', 'appreciating …' or in many cases 'being …'. This emphasises that Values are ongoing ways of being, rather than (like a goal) something that can ever be complete. More fundamentally, it's also a reminder that Values aren't strictly 'things' that – if we could peer inside your brain – we'd find sitting neatly on a shelf marked 'Values, A–Z'; they are characteristics of the ways you choose to be in this world.

- *Values are ends in themselves (more or less).*
  Being caring towards someone because it makes you popular or because you hope for a favour in return is not 'being caring' as a Value. It's when the fulfilment comes directly from the 'being caring' that we're looking at a Value. Values act as a kind of internal reward (or 'reinforcement') for actions that serve them, even if no one else notices or rewards the act – hence the use of the phrase 'ends in themselves'.

  The reason I added 'more or less' is this: a life lived according to our Values is a life well lived – in that it brings a sense of fulfilment, vitality and purpose. So in that sense they could be said to be (in part) a means to that end, if that's a kind of life that appeals to you. And it certainly does to me.

- *Values are not about happiness.*

Fulfilment isn't the same as happiness – sometimes very important and fulfilling things are difficult or sad (e.g. ensuring that someone you love has a funeral they would have approved of). And following your Values isn't always going to lead to happy outcomes; on the contrary, it can get you killed – as the fates of many a pioneer, missionary or explorer will show. But you have choices about how you serve your Value. If going to a distant and violent place to rescue children from exploitation is too risky (and maybe risking your life contravenes another Value of 'being present for my children'), then campaigning and fund-raising at home will still serve that same Value.

- *Values are not 'right' or 'wrong'.*

This is where Values as seen in ACT differ from how they might be seen in, for example, religious or political traditions. While in those latter cases, we would expect there to be clearly stated values (or maybe virtues) that followers would be encouraged to adopt because they are associated with a deity, or are seen as being right for the good of society and mankind, in ACT there are no 'good' or 'bad' Values – there are only the Values that you have. One person may hold a Value of 'being competitive', whilst another may hold the Value of 'being co-operative': each is right for that person; neither is objectively right or wrong.

If Values aren't 'right' in some absolute sense, but are instead 'right for you', then it might require some acceptance that other people hold other Values, and that could be a source of conflict; there may be no hope of changing their Values, and instead you have to find a way of dealing with that difference. And it can be hard if it suddenly becomes apparent in a relationship; but better to be clear about that difference than let it simply lurk there, making each person's actions difficult for the other to understand.

- *Values cannot all be served at the same time.*

When you start looking at using your Values to guide your choices (as we will be doing in the next chapter), you'll quickly find that actions that serve one of your Values may actively contradict another. Sometimes you are effectively choosing which Value to serve at any moment.

Since she's been attending the Coping with a Long-Term Condition course, Caroline feels she has been handling the unwanted thoughts and feelings in her life better. That doesn't mean that her physical problems have gone away, though, and at the moment she's recovering from a flare-up of her bowel condition. Most of the symptoms have gone, but she's left exhausted and knows she has to pace herself carefully for the next few days.

Unfortunately, today she's faced with a difficult choice. She is due to go with her husband to see the solicitor about the court case relating to his head injury – which she realises is in service of 'caring for those you love'. But she has also been asked to go with her daughter to take her grandson for his first day at school (serving the Value of 'nurturing those you love'). Previously she would have tried to do both in the same day, but now knows that will just make her worse.

Reluctantly, she decides that she has to go to the appointment with Geoff, as he will be unbearably stressed if they defer it. Yet having done that, she asks herself, 'So, what will I do to encourage my grandson?' and decides to get him to video-call her that evening to tell her all about his first day (even though her daughter will tell her anyway).

What Caroline has learned is that, on those occasions where you have to choose between two actions that support different Values, you then ask yourself, 'What else will I do in the service of that other Value, then?'

- *Beware of fusing with your Values.*
  Even though your Values are important, you shouldn't become too rigidly focused on them – that kind of 'fusion' can reduce your ability to react flexibly to the world and will probably mean you neglect other Values in the

process. For example, plenty of artists' biographies show how overwhelming commitment to their creativity led to a neglect of relationships that also initially mattered to them. The best advice is probably to be aware of those Values, let them guide your choices, but hold even them lightly.

7.2.5 Your Values

Having worked a little with Values, discussed what they are and aren't, and some of the ways of identifying them, it's time for you to think about how they apply to you, and 'pin down' some of your own (if you haven't already).

Exercise 7.2: Identifying your Values

You're going to write down some of your Values – at least six of them. There's a form in Appendix 1, but I also suggest you copy them into something you carry around with you – your diary, a memo on your phone or even a small piece of card in your wallet.

There are several ways to decide which are your Values:

- You may already know which Values you want to write down after reading this far, or
- you may want to look at some of the commonly occurring ones in the list I gave in section 7.2.2, or
- you may want reflect on things that you have found have brought you great fulfilment or emotional pain and work out what Values were involved in those.

Now, look at each and ask yourself, 'What have I done that lives up to that Value in the last week?'

You will undoubtedly already be living by some of your Values every day. Yet some will probably have been neglected, maybe for a long time. This is because some very important things are also difficult things to do, even when we've realised that they are what we should be doing. That will be the main subject of the next chapter.

We started this chapter by looking at the importance of a sense of purpose, and how we can lose that over time, especially given the stresses and limitations that an LTC can bring. I also quoted the great writer Viktor Frankl who, as an inmate of a concentration camp, observed those around him who survived and those who didn't. He reached the conclusion that a personal sense of meaning, purpose and direction in life was the difference between having a chance of survival or not.

I believe that if we view meaning, or purpose, in terms of being aware of our Values, and act in accordance with them, then we are likely to live a more fulfilling life, even (and maybe especially) in the face of adversity such as long-term illness.

However, knowing your Values isn't enough – it's acting on them that counts, and that is what we'll turn to now.

Key points

- Having goals and a sense of purpose can give energy and direction, and may even be good for your health.
- Though our goals may change throughout life, LTCs can get in the way of some important ones.
- It is painful to let go of cherished goals.
- We can make the mistake of letting go of goals too soon, or of holding on to them too long.
- It can be hard to find new goals when old ones are no longer realistic; try to establish why a particular goal matters by seeing which of your Values it relates to.
- It helps to know your own Values.
- Values (in this approach) are the ways you want to act in this world, what you want to stand for (e.g. 'being honest', 'being loyal', 'being caring').
- Values are ways you want to act because you think they're right for you, not because someone else wants you to.
- In the ACT approach, Values are individual; there are no Values that are absolutely 'right' or 'wrong' – your Values are your Values, and may be different from mine.

- Values will show up both in the things that bring you most fulfilment and in the things that bring you most emotional pain (when a Value is neglected or violated).
- Values are not the same as goals (that can be completed) or individual actions; they are the reason why the goal matters and a quality of how you act.
- You cannot serve all your Values at every moment; different actions will be needed to serve different Values.
- Make sure you're not continually neglecting one or more of your Values.
- Being aware of your Values, and living by them, gives a sense of purpose and fulfilment; it is a life well lived.

8

Taking action

Alina finds her long-distance chats with her friend Evka really useful. It's not simply that Evka is willing to listen to her; it's that she challenges her and doesn't let Alina simply wallow in feeling sorry for herself. In many ways, they almost become therapy sessions, which Evka doesn't mind at all, as she's got quite interested in psychology and has been doing a lot of reading around Values.

When, a few weeks ago, Alina had ended up asking 'What's the point?', Evka persuaded her to start thinking about what things matter most to her. By the end of their next call, Alina had not only a list of her Values but also a sense that things were finally about to change for the better.

Two weeks later, they speak again; Alina is demoralised, because the feel-good glow of last time has evaporated, and nothing at all has changed.

We've all seen on TV and in the movies, where a person is having psychological therapy; there will probably be a moment of insight, where they have some sudden realisation of the reason behind all their problems, and that knowledge makes everything change for the better ...

That may or may not be a good plot device to move a story on, but my experience of doing psychological therapy for real is that it very rarely works like that. There may well need to be some understanding of how things have been going wrong, and how to move forward; but there will rarely be significant and lasting improvements in a person's quality of life based on changing knowledge alone. Rather, that insight is an important first step to making changes for the better in your life; but without actually making those changes, life won't get much better.

Without action, insight doesn't help much.

8.1 How our behaviour drifts

In everyday existence too, our actions are a key part of our quality of life. If we're frequently doing things we dislike, missing out on doing things that we find fulfilling, or acting in a manner that makes us feel bad about ourselves, then we're bound to be more dissatisfied with life.

Some of the reasons for that 'drift' may be beyond our control: the requirements of a job, or family responsibilities; though if we recognise the Values that doing those things serves ('providing for my family', 'caring for those I love'), then even taxing or boring tasks can be more bearable. Not enjoyable, but bearable.

In the case of a person who has a long-term physical health problem (and remember, once we get into middle-age and beyond, that's most of us), there may be other constraints upon our actions. Some may be directly related to physical symptoms (e.g. reduced mobility, fatigue), the requirements of treatment (e.g. needing the facilities to change a colostomy bag), financial (e.g. no longer being able to hold down a well-paid job) or social (because of the limitations already listed, spending less time with friends).

> Caroline has been thinking a lot about the day she helped out at the local fete. She felt more like her old self while she was there, and although her initial reaction was to say it was no real achievement, actually it hadn't been as straightforward as it would have been years ago: she'd had to keep an eye on Geoff throughout it, rearrange seeing her grandson that day, explain (several times over) to her mother why she wasn't visiting, and generally had her routines disrupted.

More striking, though, is the realisation of how much she's been missing out on since she's given up on all this: the camaraderie and gossip, the sense of purpose in organising an event or raising money. And the feeling of being part of a community wider than her own immediate family. The needs of her family and the pressures of her own LTC have been the key reason for dropping that aspect of her life, yet the recent fete proved that actually it *is* possible to do some of that community work, especially now Geoff's a little more predictable, her grandson has started school and (following the course she went on) she's managing her IBS better.

So why, she wonders, hasn't she just been getting on with it?

As Caroline is right to realise, it's not simply external factors that cause our behaviour to drift away from what we would want it to be. There are many 'internal' tendencies that contribute to that, and if we reflect on the processes we've already discussed in this book, some of the culprits become clear:

- **Fusion** – getting caught up in long-standing thoughts about how you should or shouldn't be acting, and failing to recognise that these are just thoughts. For example, someone having the thought 'If I try studying again, I'll probably fail', and treating that thought as a reality, and so choosing not to go back to college.
- **Avoidance** – letting your behaviour be controlled by the urge to avoid feeling bad. For example, Alina giving up on a social life in order to avoid feeling embarrassment at her weight gain.
- **Short-term gains** – we are all, to different degrees, prone to taking a short-term gain even if it leads to a long-term loss. The prospect of another cup of tea and an enjoyable programme on TV (short-term gains) can easily dissuade me from getting to the gym (which is a long-term loss to my health).

- **Getting stuck in old patterns** – sometimes, habits are simply hard to break, even when you really want to act differently. You may have decided to spend more time with your family, but see an opportunity at work which will require extra evening and weekend involvement, and you may have said 'yes' before you realise it.
- **Aimless behaviour** – when someone lacks a sense of purpose, it can be hard to know which way to act; behavioural choices are more likely to be based on short-term gains or avoidance of discomfort. After all, why would someone choose to do something difficult or uncomfortable if there is no sense of purpose or longer-term goal behind it?
- **Indecision** – where we are faced with more than one possible course of action, we can get stuck in the process of decision-making. If the options are finely balanced, we can effectively be paralysed. You may know the legend of 'Buridan's ass' – a hungry and thirsty donkey who was standing exactly half-way between a pile of hay and a bucket of water, and died of hunger and thirst because there was no rational reason to choose one resource over the other.[74] I've done exactly the same when trying to choose which of two equally attractive movies to watch, and have ended up watching neither properly because I couldn't commit to one over the other.
- **Procrastination** – similar to, but distinct from, indecision; this is a more active 'putting off' process. Though it can be for many reasons, a reluctance to do the chosen action may well be at its heart, as procrastination can often be a form of experiential avoidance (avoiding whatever unwanted feeling the task would bring). Yet it often leads to discomfort of its own (regret, self-disgust), and delaying the behaviour in question may make things harder (e.g. talking to your bank about financial difficulties, visiting the dentist).

I'd argue that we all do some of the above, some of the time. And most of the time, it probably doesn't matter too much.

Sometimes, though, it does matter if we're not doing the things we would want to – if, like Alina, we know that getting back to her work and her studies, beginning to socialise again and eating a little more healthily would make her life a lot better. Or Caroline, who realises that she should get back involved in her local voluntary work, but feels too overwhelmed by her other responsibilities to make it happen.

What can ACT offer for people in these circumstances (and, to a greater or lesser extent, that's probably all of us)?

8.2 An alternative – Values-driven behaviour

The time we spent looking at Values in the last chapter wasn't an academic exercise or just for interest. It wasn't even there simply to restore a sense of purpose, because that sense of purpose only becomes worthwhile when it guides behaviour. As I said above, without action, insight doesn't help much.

The usefulness of knowing your Values comes in large part from using them to guide your actions – perhaps not exactly a 'moral compass', but a instead a 'purpose compass'.

The simplest example of that is probably when faced with a choice of actions – we can ask ourselves, 'Which Value(s) would that be serving?', much as Caroline did in the last chapter when choosing between accompanying her husband to the solicitor and going with her grandson for his first day at school. And, as she found, sometimes different Values are served by different actions. Sometimes, though, there's no real competition if you remember your Values, as Bill found when choosing to celebrate his wife's birthday rather than work extra time at the office.

In both of those cases, the person was presented with a choice, and had to make it one way or another, and awareness of Values certainly can help with that. Indeed, in ACT we'll sometimes encourage you to ask whether a certain behaviour is a move *towards* your Values, or *away* from them. My action of having a second cup of tea and watching a bit more of the cricket rather than heading for the gym would certainly count as a move 'away' from my Values around staying healthy enough to be able to contribute as much as possible to my family.

The second way that you can use your Values to guide your behaviour is when you are not presented with a forced choice, like Bill and Caroline, but rather where the initiative rests with you to do something beneficial in your life – to make your life better than it is. That includes choosing what that behaviour should be, actually getting round to it, persevering if (when?) the going gets tough, and evaluating it to be sure that it is actually having the desired effect in your life.

When Alina admits to her friend that she hasn't actually done anything with that list of Values that she'd felt good about writing, Evka is ready for what needs doing next.

'OK, Alina, so you Value "making the most of opportunities"; what are you going to actually *do* between now and when I phone you again next Thursday that's going to be an example of "making the most of opportunities"?'

Alina thinks about this, and says, 'I suppose the diploma in hotel management I've been neglecting for the last couple of months – that should be an opportunity for furthering myself, but if I don't finish this module soon, they'll kick me off. I could try getting on with that.'

With warmth in her voice as well as firmness, Evka replies, 'No – do it, or don't do it; don't say you'll "try" – that's the word we use when we're preparing an excuse for giving up.'

'OK, OK, then,' laughs Alina, 'I'll do it.'

Exercise 8.1: Values and actions

Go back to the list of your Values that you drew up in the last chapter. If you didn't get round to doing it, do so now (you won't be able to benefit from the remaining exercises unless you do).

There's a form for this in Appendix 1, or you can use a sheet of paper (or in your notebook if you've been using one), and draw up a table of five columns as shown in Figure 8.1. Label the first one **Values**, and the second one **How served in last week.** We won't be using the other three until the next exercise.

Copy in your list of Values to the first column. Now, think back carefully over the last week; try to recall specific examples of things you have done which served those Values – even though you probably weren't thinking in those terms at the time.

For example, the first rows of Alina's table might look like this:

Value	How served in last week			
Being sociable	Made video call to friend (Evka)			
Making most of opportunities	??			

Figure 8.1 Personal Values and action from Exercise 8.1 – example

She can identify one clear example of something she did that fitted (or I'd say 'served') her Value of being sociable. Notice that it's very specific – a particular thing she actually did at a particular moment, rather than a more general category of action like 'kept in touch with people'.

When she came to her Value of 'making the most of opportunities', she genuinely couldn't think of an example of something she had done in the last week that fitted in with that.

OK, now do your table. Take your time if necessary, come back and finish it after a break if needs be – but do it.

***

I'm assuming you've done the task now; so look back at what you've written, and see what you can notice about it, considering the following questions in turn:

- Were you able to identify at least one action done for every one of your Values?
- How hard was it to work out what behaviours serve what Values?
- Where were the gaps (if any) – Values that you don't think you've acted on in the last week?
- Are all your actions specific – describing identifiable things that you did at some point, rather than a vague or general impression (e.g. 'I ferried my children to and from school each day' vs 'I did lots of things for my kids')?

Maybe when you look at that table, you realise that you are already busily serving all those Values to a satisfying degree. Congratulations; that's quite an achievement, and your challenge is going to be to keep that up as time passes and circumstances change. I'd also advise making sure there's some variety in how you serve those Values – doing the same thing all the time runs the risk of it becoming a fixed behaviour pattern performed out of habit, and then you can easily stop paying attention to whether it still works or not.

Bill never minded putting lots of effort into his Carly's birthday parties – party games when she was younger, and now lots of pizza and crisps, some new DVDs and a sleep-over for her friends. It was worth it to give her happy times and encourage her to socialise.

This year, when he asks how many friends she wants over, and whether she'd like to order the DVDs to watch, Carly seems unenthusiastic. With a little questioning, she finally admits that, much as she used to love the parties when she was younger, they've seemed a bit too young for the last couple of years, only she didn't want to say anything in case it upset him or seemed ungrateful. Was there any chance that this year she could go clothes shopping with her friends and then on to the cinema instead?

For Bill, something that started as a flexible and appropriate way of serving his Value of 'nurturing those you love' became a habit, and he failed to spot when it ceased serving that Value.

Maybe, though, when you did the exercise above, there were some gaps – Values for which you couldn't say you'd done something in their service in the last week or so. That was true in Alina's example, and I'd guess it's true for most of us if we think about it carefully. Of course, when I asked you to do that exercise, there were limitations built in; there are always difficulties looking back to what you've previously done – memory has its limitations and its biases. And even if your recall was perfect, that's only a week's sample – maybe eight days ago you were fully involved in that apparently neglected Value.

Even with all those limitations acknowledged, in my experience, most of us are neglecting at least some of our Values much of the time. The good news is that, once we've realised that, we can start doing something about it.

Exercise 8.2: Values and committing to action

Now go back to that table you started in Exercise 8.1, and find one of the Values for which you hadn't found a clear action in the last week. If all of your Values had something next to them, choose a Value that you suspect you generally neglect compared with the others.

Now choose an action that you can do **within the next 48 hours** that – in however small a way – will be in service of that Value. Make sure it is realistically achievable in terms of time, resources and your abilities (e.g. 'I will go for a walk in the park', not 'I will climb Everest'). It must also be specific – so instead of 'I'll spend more time with my daughter', it could be 'I will read her a bed-time story tonight'.

Write that action in the third column of your table.

Then, as soon as possible after doing that action, write in the fourth column what you felt doing it – whether pleasant or unpleasant.

There are several possibilities for what you may have noticed in doing that exercise.

It's possible that you felt things like happiness or pride. It's also possible that the experience was difficult – hard work, either physically and/or emotionally. It's entirely possible that both were true at the same time. The point to remember is that you're not doing these activities in order to feel more happiness or less anxiety; you're doing them in order to have a more fulfilled life, a life lived according to your Values. And if it's worth doing, then you have to be willing to experience some unwanted thoughts and feelings in the pursuit of them. That's why, in the original ACT model, this wasn't just called 'action'; it was called 'committed action'.

The next step is to go back to the list and choose one (or more) of your Values and decide what you can do *within a month* that would serve it. Again, it needs to be specific, and it needs to be realistic.

And then you can continue – pick other Values for the 48-hour or one-month period. Or look at a longer-term goal – a year, maybe. Add a couple of columns to your table to enter them.

Here's Alina's table:

Value	How served in last week	Action within 48 hours	Action within one month	Action within year
Being sociable	Made video call to friend (Evka)		Organise to have some friends round to flat for supper	
Making most of opportunities	??	Phone college to check submission date for module	Complete and submit the module	Complete manage-ment course

Figure 8.2 Values and action plans from Exercise 8.2 – example

Hopefully, you've been able to see the rationale for Values-based goal-setting – why it might help you move forward in your life – and have generated some initial goals.

A quick word of warning: just check that it really is your Values that are behind your goals, rather than a familiar old story that your mind is stuck on that tries to set your direction. I've learned (eventually!) that there's a story in my mind about never really fulfilling my potential unless I'm a research academic – maybe it comes from my undergraduate education, maybe from further back. I now know that following that particular track (as vitally important as it is – the evidence for the approaches I'm writing about is mostly thanks to such people) suits me less well than what I actually do professionally – focusing on being a front-line clinician and teacher. My current role suits my Values a lot better – for example, I'm more able to act on 'being present for those I love' if I'm not forever off to conferences or meetings in other cities and other countries. That doesn't mean that I don't hear the siren call of university jobs if I see adverts for them, or that my mind doesn't criticise me for having produced so little research compared with my academic heroes. If your actions are in service of these 'old stories' in your mind rather than your living Values, then even if you do achieve them, you might not find your life getting any better.

Set your goals, then, in accordance with your Values if you want your success to make things better.

However, if you're anything like me (or most of the people I know), you will have plenty of experience of setting very reasonable and sensible goals, and then failing to achieve them. That's why we must look at some of the reasons people fail to achieve goals they've set themselves, and what can be done about that.

8.3 Barriers to action

8.3.1 Poorly set goals

What are the qualities of a goal that can actually move you forward – making it more likely you'll achieve that goal, and that achieving it will actually make your life better?

There are many books and websites offering advice about goal-setting, whether that's in relation to business, time-management, education, sport or most other areas of human activity, and it wouldn't be appropriate to rehearse all of that here. Many of them will mention the characteristics of a good goal, and may use the phrase 'SMART' or maybe 'SMARTER' goals; these are ways of remembering those characteristics, usually attributed to a writer about management called George Doran.[75] In case you're unfamiliar with this, SMART lists the initials of the qualities a goal should have. Different writers vary the wording slightly, but typically these would be:

S: specific. Is the goal a concrete description of what you will do (e.g. 'I will read to my child at least five nights out of seven this week') rather than a vague aspiration (e.g. 'I will be a better parent')?

M: measurable. How will you know when you've achieved it? Sometimes this will be in numbers ('I aim to raise £1,000 for this charity'), more often you can tell if you've achieved it in other ways ('I'll know I've got fitter if I can walk to the shop without being out of breath').

A: achievable. A goal that is unrealistic ('I will be the first person to walk on Mars') or is out of your control ('I will win the lottery') is likely to lead to failure and disappointment.

R: relevant. The goal helps you get to where you want to be (e.g. 'getting this qualification will help me get a better-paid job'); in the terms we were talking about in the last chapter, this means 'in accordance with one or more of my Values' ('getting a better-paid job matters because I Value being able to provide for my family').

T: time-framed. Saying when you aim to do this thing, or a deadline you'll have done it by (even if it's long-term). Otherwise, it can be a 'One day, I'll …' kind of dream. And the experience of significant health problems should tell us that we shouldn't keep putting off important things.

And those who use SMARTER rather than SMART would add:

E: evaluate. Take the time to check whether you have actually achieved that goal you set, or not. If you have achieved it, has it had the effects you expected, and what do you do next? If you haven't achieved it, what's happened? Did it meet all the 'SMART' criteria in the first place? Or have you fallen into one of the traps we're going to look at in the rest of the chapter?

R: re-evaluate. Particularly for more important goals in your life, it's worth checking back a few months later to see if you've maintained what you set out to achieve ('Am I still reading to my child most evenings?') or, if it was a more one-off kind of goal (e.g. gaining a qualification) whether you're really making use of it in the way you intended. This may help you decide what you need to aim for next.

So, the first set of reasons why a person may not achieve a goal may be because that goal is vague (not Specific), or you can't tell whether you achieved it or not (not Measurable), or it was unrealistic (not Achievable), or it turned out not to matter that much (not Relevant), or there was no sense of deadline or urgency (not Time-framed).

As mentioned above, these ideas have been widespread for the last few decades; they certainly weren't created within ACT or any other form of CBT (though we should draw on 'what works' from wherever it comes).

ACT does, however, have some useful things of its own to say about how we sometimes fail to achieve the things we want to, and what we can do about that.

8.3.2 Beware emotional goals

What could be more natural than wanting to be happy? Or to stop being sad?

It isn't that these aims are unnatural, unreasonable or immoral. It's just that goals that are based on achieving a particular emotional state are likely to be counterproductive. If that seems like a surprising statement, then it might be worth taking another look back at Chapter 4 on 'emotional avoidance'; basing your actions on the avoidance of unwanted emotional states will lead to narrowing your life (avoiding all social contact because it makes you anxious, avoiding relationships in case they bring sadness or loss and so on). Equally, chasing the experience of happiness can easily lead to multiple or superficial relationships (the happiness of meeting new people, new sexual relationships), drinking too much (the happiness of being mildly drunk), spending more than you can afford (the happiness of acquiring desirable things), neglecting things that are less fun but more important (the happiness of leisure), and maybe even taking heroin (which briefly provides an intense euphoria before destroying your life in a dozen ways).

Instead of emotional goals, then, you could choose Value-based goals, which are likely to give you more of a sense of fulfilment (and maybe happiness) as a side-effect of pursuing the things that matter in your life.

8.3.3 Beware setting 'dead-men's goals'

Goals seem to work better when we specify what we *will* rather than what we *won't* do. Instead of 'I won't shout when my wife doesn't understand my physical limitations', we could aim for 'I will explain calmly when she misunderstands, even if I'm feeling wound up inside'. Specifying what behaviour you *will* do gives you a clearer thing to aim at (and be SMARTER about, if you're using those principles).

The easy way to remember this is to ask whether you're setting a 'dead-man's goal': something that could be performed to perfection by a dead person. A dead person will not smoke this week, or eat fatty snacks, or shout at their partner, or …

You could ask, though, what about those situations where your goal really is, say, to *not* eat unhealthy snacks – both a dead-man's goal and an important one for your health? Well, a better alternative would be to specify an active goal, such as 'When I feel a craving for an unhealthy snack, I will simply carry on with whatever I was doing and let the craving sit there until it goes away'. Or maybe 'When I feel the craving, I'll have a glass of water/piece of fruit/healthy alternative instead, even though my mind will be telling me how much better a chocolate digestive would taste'.

8.3.4 Don't tell yourself you'll 'try'

I've mentioned this principle earlier in the book, as did Alina's friend Evka. When we tell ourselves that we'll 'try' to do something, we're generally setting ourselves up for not doing it, or for failing. I'll *try* to get to that retirement party; this year I'll really *try* to keep in touch with my friends better.

We need to be careful here, since language always brings complexities, and how we use the word 'try' is no exception, because one use of it is perfectly fine: if we're talking about doing something with the intention of making something happen, but where the success of the action cannot be guaranteed. I can try to mend a bicycle puncture, work hard to the best of my limited experience; whether it works is only partly within my control. That sense of 'try' is OK.

However, when we're talking not about outcomes but about our own actions, then 'try' may not be OK. If a more technophobic friend asks if I can help in getting their computer to work properly with its printer, then as I've already said I can work hard with no guarantee of success – so it would be OK for me to say, 'I'll *try* to fix it for you.' However, if I say, 'I'll *try* to take a look at it this evening', then I'm talking about my own actions, which are under my own control; so, I'd be better off saying, 'I will take a look at it today, though I can't promise I'll be able to fix it.' Saying 'I'll try to take a look' opens the gate for never quite getting round to taking a look.

So how would that difference look in terms of LTCs? That while it would be reasonable to say, 'I'll try to keep working until the kids are through college', it would be poor goal-setting to say, 'I'll try to take fatigue-management more seriously from now on.' I either start working at my fatigue-management or I don't – in that sense there is no 'try'.

Therefore, unless you're talking about outcomes rather than your own actions, don't tell yourself or others that 'you'll try to ...'. Say what you're going to do, then do it, however successful or otherwise it turns out to be.

8.3.5 'But it feels bad ...'

I think this is one of the biggest unacknowledged reasons why well-motivated people, with the appropriate skills, fail to achieve their well-thought-out goals.

A few years ago, Caroline found herself getting into a terrible state. She was always rushing around, doing things for everyone because they always seemed to ask her rather than someone else. Of course they did; she was good at getting things done, and would always says 'yes' if you explained how important it was!

However, though she'd smile and get on with organising that event, giving a lift to someone or writing the annual report, inside she'd often be fuming because of all the things of her own that she wanted to get on with, but was too busy or too tired to after doing what others wanted. And somehow, when *she* needed help, people were never quite so quick to agree. At times, she'd get angry and tearful at home, and once in a while she'd snap in public, but then feel terribly ashamed and go back to trying to please everyone, and avoid upsetting people at any cost – even if that person was a waiter who'd brought her a plate of food that had been badly overcooked.

In the end, her husband Geoff – supportive and insightful before he had his accident – persuaded her to go to an assertiveness training class being run at the local college. Although she was very nervous at first, she actually quite enjoyed it and learned lots of useful techniques to help her stand up for herself appropriately (without being aggressive) and not let others exploit her. She enjoyed the fact that the classes discussed actual skills, like how to state your needs and requests clearly without apologising for them, deal with hostility, negotiate an outcome that suits both parties, politely and persistently refuse to give in, and how to back-track if you've slipped up and agreed to something that you now realise you can't – or don't want to – do.

> She found that she could see the point of these easily and, when she practised them with one of her classmates, could usually find the right words.
>
> The problem was that, if an opportunity to be assertive cropped up between classes – even something as clear-cut as sending back a restaurant meal that was badly overcooked – she ended up not using all those new techniques.
>
> 'I could see what was going on, and how I ought to handle it,' she told the tutor the following week, 'but the prospect of actually doing it made me feel so anxious and awkward that it was just easier to put up with it. Well, at the time it was; afterwards, of course, I hated myself for being so weak again.'

Earlier in my career I would often be working with people who needed to develop the skills Caroline was learning; and the sorts of ideas and techniques I suggested could really help someone to follow the advice of a very useful self-help book of the time and 'Don't say "yes" when you want to say "no"'.[76] Yet, as useful as some of these skills were (and I found myself using them a lot too), many of the people I was seeing were failing to put them into practice – not because they didn't know *what* to do, but because actually doing it made them feel bad. Bad as in anxious, guilty or embarrassed. And as we have seen time and again in this book, the urge to avoid feeling bad is strong; the temporary relief of avoiding feeling bad is very reinforcing (meaning it makes you more likely to do the same thing in the future), and later comes the huge price of doing so: realisation that you've missed out again on something that mattered to you, sacrificed another chance for moving forwards, and a poorer view of yourself. Plus, ironically, you're likely to feel bad about yourself.

The key to success is both to acquire any skills or techniques you lack and then to learn to accept the temporary feelings of anxiety, embarrassment or whatever as the price you need to pay to follow the path that's right for you. Also, remember that you'll gain more in the long term by taking this short-term discomfort.

I've spent a while talking about assertiveness here, but hopefully you'll have noticed that this is a much more general point; any of the goals we want to pursue may involve discomfort along the way – maybe emotional discomfort, maybe physical. If we allow ourselves to get de-railed by avoiding discomfort, then we imprison ourselves in a 'comfort zone': a cage defined by the limits of what we can do without feeling bad in any way. And the walls of that kind of cage tend to get smaller and smaller (ask anyone who has developed agoraphobia), so its status as a 'safe place' is an illusion anyway.

If a goal is worth achieving, it will be worth experiencing some unwanted thoughts, feelings or sensations en route; refusal to accept those will limit your life.

When the type of 'feeling bad' we are talking about is anxiety, there is one complication; very high anxiety levels can be so overwhelming as to interfere with thoughts and actions. It might actually be too much to ask someone with an acute fear of heights to go straight to standing at the top of the Eiffel Tower and accepting the presence of their overwhelming, blinding panic. They might need a programme of gradually building up to something that extreme (looking out of an upstairs window, being at the top of a moving staircase, looking out from a shopping centre balcony and so on). This is similar to a well-established[77] treatment approach for phobias called 'graded exposure' or 'systematic desensitisation'; however, whereas you would traditionally attempt to use relaxation skills to cope with each stage, or alternatively wait until the anxiety burned itself out, you may not be surprised to hear me say that ACT has a slightly different idea. At each stage, the goal is not to get rid of the anxiety (actively or passively), but rather to practise allowing it to be there, and noticing that – even with it present – the world does not end, and you *can* carry on in a direction that matters to you.

This might also be the moment to mention the idea of 'willpower'. One of the things your mind may tell you when you consider doing something that is important and difficult (and especially when you are considering giving up on it!) is 'I don't have enough willpower for this'. I've certainly experienced that, and the idea of willpower as a thing that different people may have in different amounts is widespread in society.

It is certainly true that some people are more prone to put up with temporary discomfort in order to gain a greater reward, and this tendency can show up life-long;[78] you may have heard terms like 'deferred gratification' and 'impulse control' used in this context. The difficulty comes if we accept that willpower is a thing that we have, in large or small amounts, that somehow determines our ability to stick to something that is difficult and important (a healthy eating plan, a course of study, stopping smoking), rather than doing something easier or with more immediate gratification (give up on the study and watch TV instead, eat the fried breakfast rather than the muesli). If we buy that view of things, then failure to follow through on goals is out of our control – it's just down to how much or little willpower we've got, and our mind will have a ready excuse for taking the easier-in-the-short-term path.

If we are going to use the term 'willpower' (and maybe we're better avoiding it altogether), better to see it not as a thing you have but as something you do; carry on towards a goal you Value, even in the presence of uncomfortable experiences, unhelpful thoughts and urges to give up, and do something easier. And that's exactly what we've been talking about throughout this book.

So beware when your mind starts telling you a story about how much willpower you don't have; your choice is still the same – do this thing and have any unwanted experiences that may come with it, or don't do it, avoid the unwanted experiences and move no further forward in the things that matter to you. Your choice. Talking about 'willpower' is irrelevant.

8.3.6 'I just can't be bothered'

We've all had times when we know what we should be doing, and kind-of want to get on with, but we don't get on with it because we just can't get started. It's so much easier just to sit here a bit longer, and I'll definitely do it later. Or tomorrow. Yes, absolutely a new start tomorrow …

It may be that the goal wasn't set properly – if the thing you're telling yourself to do isn't actually doable, or doesn't actually matter to you, then your lack of application to it makes sense. So if it's this thing specifically that you can't be bothered to do (but you're as motivated as usual in other areas of your life), then it's worth checking whether the goal is a SMART one, that you've identified which of your Values it serves, and then get ready to put up with whatever unwanted experience it will take (boredom, effort, anxiety, etc.). And just do it.

Sometimes, though, the problem isn't with the specific goal, but with the state you've got into that affects lots of areas of activity. Someone who has been experiencing long periods of low mood (that might be labelled 'depression') may find themselves becoming less and less active generally. Getting started can become harder, and even everyday activities can seem like mountains to climb.

At its worst, this kind of withdrawn inactivity can be hugely disabling and lead to self-neglect (cooking a meal, having a shower or even getting out of bed). Realistically, if you were in that situation, you probably wouldn't be reading this book – or at least you wouldn't have got this far. This is the point (if it persists) at which someone needs professional support; most likely their family doctor in the first instance, but there should really be input from a mental health or psychological care professional. Some would argue that anti-depressant medication should play a part in treatment; I'd argue that, at the very least, any medication should be used alongside an appropriate psychological therapy, and certainly not instead of it.

One of the psychological treatments for this kind of state is called Behavioural Activation,[79] and while it would be hard to self-administer for someone in a very serious state of inactivity, we can use some of its core principles ourselves if we just feel in a bit of a rut, or are finding it hard to get ourselves going with those activities that matter. Here are some guidelines.

Get in the habit of taking action:

- Remember your Values.
- Make sure that the activities you'd like to re-start are in service of these Values, or at least compatible with them.
- Divide each day into three segments (morning, afternoon, evening). In each segment do one extra planned activity (in addition to what you're already doing).
- Aim small (maybe just a couple of minutes' worth of action), but make sure you actually do those things; for example, it's better to start with 5 minutes of exercise that you actually *do* than an hour of exercise that you don't.
- Don't give yourself excuses for not doing the thing; if something genuinely crops up and prevents you doing it, then you'll have *two* to do in the next segment of the day – where there's reluctance, don't reward avoidance.
- The goal is to get into the habit of taking action – not spending too much time thinking about it, reflecting on how you feel or giving yourself reasons for not doing it.
- Getting busy with small, achievable things will make you more ready and able to take systematic action on bigger things that matter.

8.3.7 Others get in the way

Humans are very social beings. The majority of our goals are going to involve other people to some degree or other. The decision to eat fresh fruit rather than cake may sound as if only you and your kitchen cupboard are involved; until, that is, you visit your aunt and she serves a Victoria sponge she's just baked with tea and simply won't take 'no' for an answer.

Harder still, if we're talking about healthier eating (a vital part of minimising the impact of so many LTCs), is trying to improve your diet whilst being responsible for providing meals to a family who don't want to change their own eating patterns; it's hard to stick to salad while cooking sausage and mash.

We can, it's true, get better at explaining what we want from other people, attempt to persuade them, stand up for ourselves in an assertive manner, and they might help us with our goals, or at least not stand in our way. However, there's no guarantee of that, because of this central principle:

We cannot control the behaviour of another human; we can attempt to influence it, but we cannot control it.

And what goes with that fact is this one:

There is only one person whose behaviour *is* under your control, and that is you.

So while we will try to get others on our side where necessary, there will be some times when we just have to accept that their choices are their choices, and focus back on our own behaviour. That fits in with some of the SMART goal-setting we looked at before – these kind of goals should be about what *you* are going to do, not what you hope others are going to do. That still can include attempting to influence others, because the attempt is your behaviour, so long as you recognise that the outcome is not entirely under your control.

Watch out, though, that you're not using their (real) disagreement with what you're doing as an excuse for stopping, when what you might actually be doing is simply avoiding the discomfort of possible confrontation arising from you saying where you stand on this issue. As always, the question is not whether confrontation is in its nature right or wrong, but rather 'Which course of action takes me towards my Values?'

Bill has tried to be open with his daughters Carly and Rebecca about his MS. He wants them to treat it as a matter of fact: something that he has to adapt to and will sometimes affect their lives too – for example, when he can't take part in the fathers' race at school sports day. But he also believes it shouldn't stop them doing most of the things they want. He's been determined never to treat it as a secret or a tragedy, something he finds easier himself since learning how to defuse from his thoughts. And, fortunately, his wife Trish has exactly the same attitude.

Unfortunately, the same is not true of his older sister Sue; she views the MS as some sort of death sentence, still gets tearful when talking about it, and is forever bringing him news of some new quack remedy she's read about in a tabloid or on the internet. Worst of all, she occasionally talks that way in front of the girls.

It comes to a head one Christmas, when, after a few glasses of wine, she emotionally tells Carly and Rebecca to look after their father, pray for him, and that they'll always be welcome to stay with her if Daddy has one of his 'attacks'.

As much as Bill loves his sister and realises she means well, he knows Trish is right when she tells him he'll have to confront Sue about this behaviour once she sobers up. He's going to hate doing it, because Sue never takes criticism well and is bound to be angry, and if she does come to understand what she has done, she'll then be overwhelmed with guilt, which is even harder to put up with. If this was just about his own annoyance, then he'd probably let it go. But this is about Rebecca and Carly's ability to deal with their father's condition, and about managing its impact on their childhood; and what Sue's doing might well harm that.

So he's willing to experience the anxiety, the guilt and the anger that will no doubt ensue from challenging her if that's what it takes to protect his girls ...

Before we finish looking at the roles of others – and especially families and friends – it's important to remember that they are often your biggest support, and may well be a more important reason for you trying to manage your health than your own personal well-being. While I've discussed the problems of them 'getting in the way' of the action you want to take, much of the time they can help more than hinder – particularly if they understand why you're attempting to do things the way you are. Interference may come from their concern for your well-being, either based on not understanding what's good for you, or (we must consider) based on seeing a risk you haven't recognised in what you're planning to do. Either way, communication is likely to help.

Bill does have the conversation with Sue, and, as he expected, she is initially angrily defensive and then full of remorse and self-loathing for being a terrible sister and aunt. Later, though still a little tearful, she does explain some of her thinking:

'You're right, Bill – I was out of line and of course it's your decision how to handle this for those lovely girls. It's just that ... Carly was talking to me earlier in the day and – completely unprompted – said that one of the hardest things about your condition was that it felt like everyone had to be so positive all the time. She said it was hard to say she was worried for you, had read some scary things on the internet about MS, and wondered what would happen to her and Rebecca if you had a bad attack and Trish was busy looking after you.'

That gives Bill something to think about, and they agree that maybe it would have been better if Sue had come to him after talking to Carly. As awkward as it has been, confronting Sue has been helpful in more than one way.

8.3.8 'My condition stops me achieving my goals'

Alina would have to admit that she's been feeling a bit better since being back at work. What's more, she's getting some sense of achievement from getting on with her hotel management course.

Her mood takes a tumble, though, when she finds a 'Long-term Goal' assignment she had written at the beginning of the management course, where she describes managing a sports and health spa. She had also included details of how she intended to pursue 'fitness instructor' qualifications alongside hotel management ones, as holding both sets of skills would put her in a stronger position to develop such a business.

Even though she has been managing and living with her fibromyalgia much better lately, she knows that the chances of getting back into peak physical fitness – let alone training as an instructor –– are remote. After all, a serious pain flare-up would be more devastating to that work than to general hotel management.

She realises that, through no fault of her own, here's one goal she's going to have to let go of.

As I said at the beginning of the book, long-term physical health conditions put real limitations on people – there's no way of coping or of thinking that changes that fact. For most people with such a condition, some goals that might otherwise have been realistic become unrealistic. And letting go of a cherished goal can be hard, as was discussed in the last chapter, so it will involve experiencing some strong emotions and difficult thoughts.

Remember, though, what we have learned about the role of Values in goal-directed behaviour; the goal matters because it serves an important Value, yet Values are not tied to specific goals. So we go back to the man in Chapter 7 who dearly wanted to teach his son to fish; his LTC meant he couldn't, and that was a genuine loss. Yet by examining the Values underpinning the importance of that goal, he was able to find an alternative that served the same Values.

So, when your condition genuinely does prevent you attaining a goal, you need to find a different goal that serves the same Value, yet is realistic given your actual situation.

Slightly trickier is the *uncertainty* that comes with many LTCs. If you knew for certain exactly how much energy you'd have on a given day, and how long it would last, then you could always make plans accordingly, because you'd know for sure whether or not you'd be able to – for example – go for the big day out in town that your friends are planning. But we all know that's generally not how it works; neither you nor your healthcare team will be able to predict how you'll feel a month from now. Certainly, you can take all the measures that increase your chance of being OK – not do anything over-taxing in the couple of days before, plan rests into the day, make sure you're eating and drinking the right amounts of the right things and so on – but you still can't be certain how well you'll be.

Occasionally (and understandably enough), people respond to this by giving up on planning ahead; you can't say 'yes' to that day out because you can't know if you'll be able to go. The same might go for planning a holiday or committing to a family Christmas gathering. It sounds extreme, but people do gradually drift into this state, and the costs are clear: many important things (about new experiences, about family togetherness, about community involvement, about fun) just disappear. And life becomes about getting through each day, hoping tomorrow will be better, and if it is ... then not necessarily doing much with it.

The alternative is – as ever – acceptance: acceptance that sometimes you won't be able to do things *and* not letting that get in the way of doing what you can. Making plans not with a rose-tinted expectation that everything will be fine, but rather with the knowledge that you might be feeling OK, or you might not.

Basically, it's better to make plans, and sometimes have to cancel them, than never to plan anything.

There are things you can do to make planning more successful given this uncertainty:

- If others are involved, let them know what your concerns are; otherwise they may simply assume you're not keen on the idea at all. If they know in advance, you're less likely to feel guilty if you have to withdraw at the last minute.
- Think about 'the most reversible choice'; if you have several options (e.g. of where to go on a short holiday), but there is a concern that you may have to pull out at short notice, then it makes sense to find out if there are any hotel options where there's no cost for a late cancellation.
- Don't just hope it will go well; think through likely problems that may arise (e.g. 'I have a migraine', 'I don't have a migraine, but I'm really tired because I'm recovering from one') and work out what you would do in each case ('Our accommodation needs to be central so I can easily get back to lie down', 'I'll rest in the café while the others

tour the museum'). Even these plans may have to be varied, but the very act of thinking ahead this way makes it much more likely that a person will successfully do the things they aim to. In fact, this approach of 'conditional planning' (or 'implementation intentions') is a good way of increasing your chance of sticking to all sorts of plans and behaviour change.[80]

The theme of this chapter has been action. Thinking about things and feeling things are unlikely in themselves to end up with you living a better life – they might be necessary, but I'd argue they're rarely sufficient. At the end of the day, you've got to do something if you want your life to get better in the presence of an LTC. Or, actually, if you haven't got an LTC; the same thing's true.

So what are you doing now?

Exercise 8.3: Doing it

Go back to the Values-based action table you drew up in Exercise 8.2. Now that you've read about some of the barriers to action, and ways around them, do the goals you listed – for action within 48 hours, for action within one month, for action within the year – still seem the right ones? Change them if necessary.

Think about possible problems that may arise, and what you would need to do then ('conditional planning').

And then?

Then 'JFDI': Just Flippin' Do It!

Key points

- Without action, insight isn't much help; it's not enough to understand your difficulties – you have to act on them.
- Our actions can drift away from what we would want them to be for both practical and psychological reasons.
- Practical barriers to effective action for a person with an LTC may include physical limitations, treatment effects, financial impact and social disadvantage.

- Psychological reasons include fusion, avoidance, the dominance of short-term gains, lack of direction, indecision and procrastination.
- If you base your actions on your Values, you know your goals will genuinely matter to you, and you can spot areas of your life you've been neglecting.
- Other barriers to effective action include poorly set goals (remember SMARTER goals), setting emotional goals, dead-men's goals, just 'trying', avoiding feeling bad, lethargy and others getting in the way. They can all be overcome.
- We cannot control the behaviour of another human; we can attempt to influence it, but we cannot control it.
- There is only one person whose behaviour is under your control, and that is you.

9

Putting it together

Over the last eight chapters, we've looked at a range of ways in which people are affected psychologically by their LTCs:

- How easy it is to become stuck in a struggle with your thoughts, feelings, urges and physical experiences, trying to control them or avoid them, but actually just making things worse.
- How we become tangled up, or 'fused', with distressing thoughts.
- How avoidance of feeling bad ('experiential avoidance') can lead us to narrowing our lives.
- How getting lost in the past and the future, and not paying attention to the present, can prevent you from making the most of your situation.
- How getting stuck inside an old story about 'who I am' can get in the way of moving forward.
- How losing a sense of purpose and direction due to the changes in your life can make it harder to gain fulfilment in life.
- How failing to act, or to act effectively, will leave you stuck in a hole.

These things are, I'd argue, universals – they affect all humans no matter what their health, finances, social setting or popularity. Yet we're here to discuss the impact of LTCs, and the people we've been following encountered all of those problems. Alina found herself avoiding her world because of how she'd changed, and for a while lost all direction. Bill's natural problem-solving mind got him into trouble when the problem couldn't be solved, leaving him with hours of worrying. Caroline wasn't as able to deal with her own health problems or her husband's care needs because of her tendency to take on too much, to avoid asserting herself, and then become angry and embittered. And Desmond was so devastated at the loss of his strength and fitness that he gave up on all the things that had mattered to him.

Over the chapters, we've looked at ways of making sense of these kinds of problems and doing things differently, as suggested by the form of CBT called ACT.

The thing to notice is that these aren't just a long list of entirely separate suggestions, but actually link together; hence the number of times you'll have read in this book 'as we saw in the previous chapter' or 'we'll go into that in more depth in the next chapter'.

I've not gone into all the technical and 'geeky' theoretical and philosophical reasons underneath the way these elements fit together. There are good books available if you do want to go more into the underpinnings of all this.[81,82] Within ACT, though, we're very keen on the principle of 'what moves us forward' being more important than 'what is absolutely true', so fortunately we have ways of putting the elements together that are more useable.

In this book, I've followed one of the conventions in ACT (and there are others) of splitting the key problems and the key approaches into six main areas. So, naturally enough, when we put those together we get a hexagon.[83] Actually, we can have two hexagons – one representing the 'problem' processes, one representing the 'helpful' processes that oppose them.

Here's the 'problem' hexagon (see Figure 9.1), which reflects the processes that can lead to being stuck in your suffering.

And here is its opposite (see Figure 9.2), the hexagon of approaches that can help you get 'unstuck' by responding more flexibly to your thoughts, feelings and experiences, and so get you moving forward again.

This helps us see how closely these processes are linked and the elements they have in common; the skills of just noticing what thoughts and feelings are present (rather than

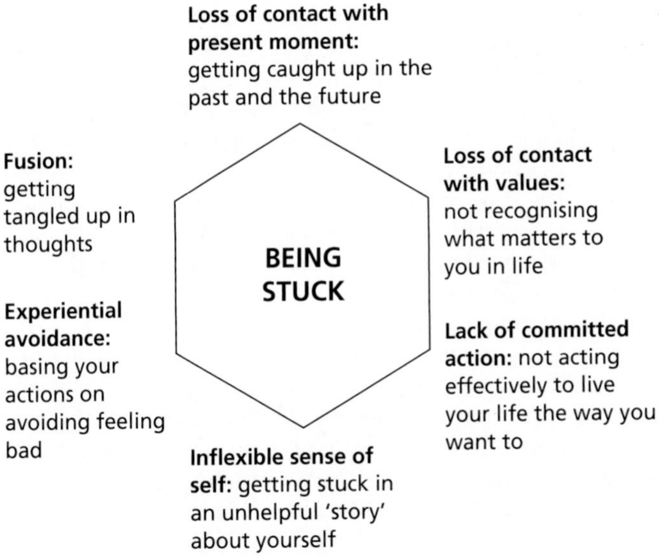

Loss of contact with present moment: getting caught up in the past and the future

Fusion: getting tangled up in thoughts

Experiential avoidance: basing your actions on avoiding feeling bad

BEING STUCK

Loss of contact with values: not recognising what matters to you in life

Lack of committed action: not acting effectively to live your life the way you want to

Inflexible sense of self: getting stuck in an unhelpful 'story' about yourself

Figure 9.1 The 'problem' hexagon

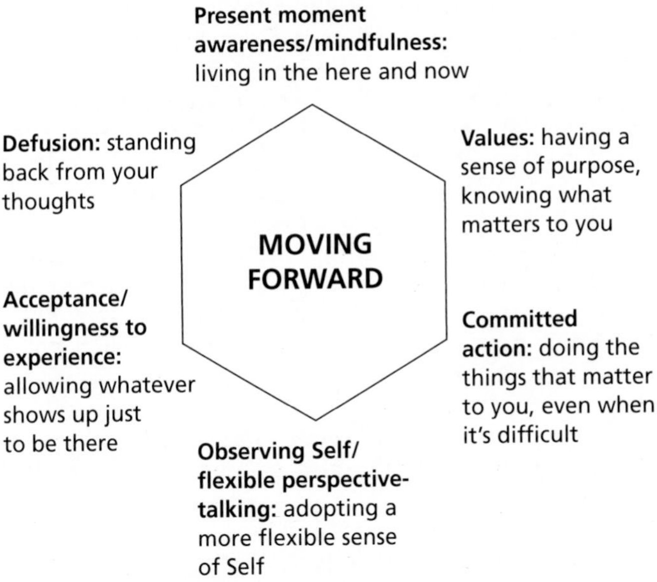

Present moment awareness/mindfulness: living in the here and now

Defusion: standing back from your thoughts

Acceptance/ willingness to experience: allowing whatever shows up just to be there

MOVING FORWARD

Values: having a sense of purpose, knowing what matters to you

Committed action: doing the things that matter to you, even when it's difficult

Observing Self/ flexible perspective-talking: adopting a more flexible sense of Self

Figure 9.2 The hexagon of ways forward

letting them take over) are also part of 'present moment awareness'. That present moment awareness involves taking the 'Observing Self' perspective. When we move forward with committed action, we will experience unwanted thoughts and feelings which will require us to defuse and be willing to accept their presence. And so on. We don't actually need to work out what all of those links are; we only need to notice that each of those approaches strengthens the others. Whatever element we are using, the others make it more manageable and more likely to move us forward.

The ultimate goal of all this is a life well lived, even with whatever circumstances show up (e.g. long-term health problems); and as I've said before, a life well lived is a life lived according to your Values. It will not always bring you ease or happiness or freedom from all distress; it should bring you a sense of fulfilment and vitality, so long as you're paying enough attention in the present moment to notice it.

The precise details of what a life well lived will look like for you will depend on the person you are – especially the Values you hold dear – and upon the circumstances you find yourself in, including those dictated by your health.

I think this is a profoundly hopeful message – that this approach is not just about minimising the negatives of life (being less sad, less stressed), but about getting more of what you want (Value) out of it, in the presence of whatever circumstance gives you, including but not limited to an LTC. This way, your life doesn't have to just be about coping with your health.

At the end of the last chapter, I stated that action has to be at the heart of moving forward (or even of not slipping further backwards). It is about what you *do*.

So, simpler even than our hexagons, we can boil down ACT to its essence:

I will do ... [action], in the service of ... [Value], and am willing to experience ... [unwanted thoughts and feelings] if that's what it takes.

For Alina, this could be:

'I will start going out with friends again, in the service of being sociable (and maybe being in a special relationship), and am willing to experience anxiety and self-consciousness about my appearance if that's what it takes.'

For Bill:

'I will spend more time relaxing and talking with my children, in the service of nurturing them, and am willing to experience distressing thoughts and images about the future when they ask about my illness, if that's what it takes.'

For Caroline:

'I will say "No" to inconvenient requests from others in the service of self-care and being more available to Geoff, and am willing to experience feelings of guilt and thoughts about letting people down if that's what it takes.'

For Desmond:

'I will pace myself and use a wheelchair when necessary, in the service of still being actively involved in family life and loyalty to my old comrades, and am willing to experience a sense of resentment and reminders that I'm not the man I used to be if that's what it takes.'

In each case, the willingness to accept the presence of unwanted thoughts and feelings (and remember, 'willing' isn't the same as 'wanting'!) will require some mindfulness/present moment awareness, and the ability to observe what is happening inside and outside yourself at that moment rather than getting tangled up in it.

And what happens when you get stuck again, or drift back into old habits, or find yourself blocked by some new development in your condition or elsewhere in your life?

Just go back to the basic principles. Look at the 'problem' hexagon and ask whether you're fusing with thoughts, avoiding experiences, losing contact with the present moment, getting stuck in a story about yourself, losing sight of your Values, or whether you've set the wrong goal or aren't committing to pursuing it.

Then look at the second hexagon, and decide where you should focus your effort: practising defusion, or acceptance of experience, mindfulness, changing your perspective, focusing on your Values or pursuing committed action in service of those Values. It's probably some of each. And then go back to the chapter of this book devoted to that area.

Is it easy? Of course not. But it is possible to make life better than it has been, even with a long-term physical health condition.

And …

… it only works if you actually do it.

So do it!

Key points

- To move on from being stuck in a struggle with your experiences, the core actions are to practise defusion from thoughts, acceptance of experience, present moment awareness, changing your perspective, focusing on your Values and taking committed action in support of those Values.
- Each element of that approach is connected to, and involves, the others.
- At a simpler level, we can commit to the following: 'I will do … [action], in the service of … [Value], and am willing to experience … [unwanted thoughts and feelings] if that's what it takes'.
- If you do that, life – even with an LTC – can be better than it is now.

10

Conclusion

All-out war, or living with the enemy?

In the years leading up to 1920, for a variety of reasons, the widespread and excessive consumption of alcohol was seen as major problem in the United States of America. The 18th Amendment was passed in January of that year, banning its production and sale, and introducing the era of Prohibition. Already one of the most powerful countries in the world, the USA had indentified alcohol consumption as an enemy and had gone to war with it.

Within ten years it was clear that war had not just been ineffective, but had caused new problems: vast amounts of revenue left the legitimate economy and taxation system and instead boosted the development of organised crime. Violent crime rose sharply as bootlegging gangs fought turf wars. People carried on drinking, but in unregulated bars with smuggled alcohol of dubious quality and safety. Large amounts of money were spent on enforcement of prohibition, but this was undermined by bribery from the profits of organised crime. What started as an attempt to decrease society's problems and improve morality managed, according to some historians, to spread bribery, violence, cynicism and immorality from the gangsters of the underworld to the highest office in the land.[84] In 1933, a further Amendment was passed to bring Prohibition to an end.

Whether you agree with the principle or the reasoning behind it or not (and I write as someone fond of a glass of red wine or pint of bitter), in practice Prohibition was a disaster.

Even when something is clearly causing harm, there is danger in committing to all-out war on it that you will ultimately be unsuccessful *and* end up losing more than you gain in the process.

Few who have actual experience of long-term physical conditions would argue that they aren't a bad thing; yes, they may be the trigger to changing your priorities and could even (possibly, with help of this book) force you to connect more closely with your Values, but overall they are a malign influence in our lives. They bring limitations, loss, frustrations, physical suffering and mental anguish for the person with the condition and for those who love them. An LTC is never going to be your friend, and that's absolutely not what we're aiming for here. Strictly speaking, it can't literally be your enemy, as that would imply it intended to harm you, and any physical condition is simply a collection of unwanted physical processes – it has no mind and so cannot intend anything.

As a metaphor, though, an LTC certainly can feel like an enemy; yet that doesn't mean it's wise to go to war with it any more than it was wise for the USA to go to war with alcohol. Now, in some acute conditions, a war is exactly what's called for; with certain forms of leukaemia, a brutal chemotherapy regime stands a chance of defeating the disease outright. Even within LTCs that can never actually be cured as such, a specific symptom or problem might be brought under control or even eliminated by some intervention.

Things that can be changed should be changed – so long as the cost of that change doesn't exceed the benefit.

However, many aspects of LTCs can't be defeated or significantly changed – that's pretty much what defines them as long-term. And in these cases, a war runs the risk of becoming all-consuming and unending, and while it grinds on, your life isn't moving forward.

This is why I called this book *Living with the Enemy*; when we learn to co-exist, to work hard in defending ourselves where necessary, yet remain determined to put most energy into moving forward with a life we Value, even though the enemy is still there, causing trouble – that's really winning.

And the techniques in this book can help you do that.

As we'll see when we find out where the four people who we've been following end up a couple of years later.

Caroline is enjoying life a lot more. She's become more able to say 'no' to people, so finds herself under less time-pressure. This seems in turn to have helped with her bowel problem. It still flares up occasionally, but that's rare, and she takes time to look after herself properly when it does. She's also able to deal better with Geoff's behaviour; her mind still occasionally tries to tell her one of the old stories about it being unfair and too much to manage, but she's able to let those thoughts go and focus back on the needs of the man she still loves, and actually enjoy his company. Most of the time, anyway.

Two years on, Bill's MS has worsened a little; he has less stamina, especially in hot weather, and has had to reduce his hours a little at work. That's meant a few economies, but nothing terrible yet. And because he's spending far less time worrying about the future, he's more able to enjoy the things that are still OK. Being less panicky about the future himself, he's now more able to allow his daughters to voice any worries they have. And, predictably, that's meant that they very rarely have anything they need to ask, focusing instead on the normal concerns of girls their age.

Desmond, sadly, died a year ago. His lung condition continued to deteriorate, and the strain on other systems within his body became too much. A few months before he died, though, he was able to take part in a Remembrance Sunday parade in uniform, wearing his medals, being pushed in a wheelchair by a younger veteran. He had felt some embarrassment at first, it's true, but that was soon overtaken by pride, sadness for those being remembered and a powerful sense of belonging, which mattered more to him than anything.

And Alina is doing very well indeed. After completing her hotel management course, she's working at a bigger and better establishment. There's more desk and computer work than standing, which helps a little with managing her fibromyalgia. The pain still occurs, more at some times than others, and she has to balance rest with keeping active, but she hasn't needed a day off work since starting there.

Outside work, things are even better; she can't exercise intensively, but, by eating more sensibly and gradually increasing her activity, she has lost some weight. She's enjoying a social life again and has even started a relationship that seems to be going well. Of course, she still catches herself thinking she's unattractive, or wanting to avoid being out and about, but she's learned to just let those thoughts and feelings be, and keep moving forward anyway. Her pains won't let her forget that she's got an LTC, but that's no longer what she's about. She's too busy getting on with living.

And if you apply what you've read in this book, you should be able to get on with living too.

Appendix 1

Notes on exercises

There are several exercises in this book, and in order to benefit I've strongly suggested the reader undertakes each of them. While some are completed with just a few minutes' thought, some require many days or weeks of practice. Depending how quickly you are reading the book, it is quite possible that you will end up working on a new exercise whilst still completing a previous longer-term one.

Here is a table of how that might work out if you were to be moving through the book at the rate of – for example – two chapters a week (and you could, of course, be reading faster or slower than that).

Week	1	2	3	4	5	
Exercise						
2.1	x					
2.2	x					
2.3	x					
3.1		x				
3.2		x	x			
3.3				x		

Week	1	2	3	4	5	
Exercise						
3.4					x	
3.5		x				
4.1		x				
4.2		x				
4.3		x	x			
5.1			x			
5.2			x			
5.3			x	x		
5.4			x			
5.5			x	x		
6.1			x			
6.2			x			
7.1				x		
7.2				x		
8.1				x		
8.2 and 8.3				x	x	**Rest of year!**

Figure A1.1 When you might be working on different exercises – example

Exercise 2.1 (Chapter 2): Alina's hot cross bun

This is one way that we could complete the 'hot cross bun' for Alina in this exercise:

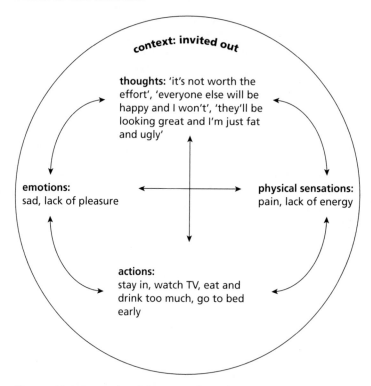

Figure A1.2 Example of 'hot cross bun' from Exercise 2.1

Exercise 2.2 (Chapter 2): Thinking about your reactions

Complete your own hot cross bun:

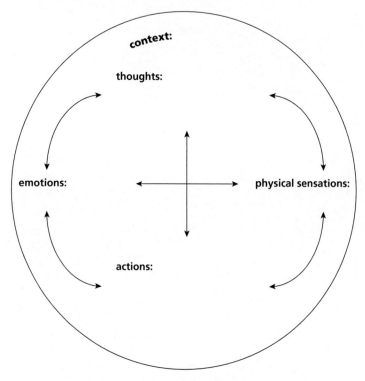

Figure A1.3 'Hot cross bun' model of how people react

Exercise 2.3 (Chapter 2): How you've attempted to deal with problems

Problem:		
How I've tried handling it	**SHORT-TERM effect**	**LONG-TERM effect**

Figure A1.4 Ways of coping and their effects from Exercise 2.3

Exercise 3.1 (Chapter 3): Noticing what thoughts come

What came into my mind (e.g. thoughts, distractions, urges, feelings)

Figure A1.5 Experiences during Exercise 3.1

Exercise 4.1 (Chapter 4): What feelings show up?

Date/time	Name of emotion	Physical sensations noticed	Situations occurs in
26 Feb, 3.30 p.m.	Anxiety	Knot in stomach, tension across shoulders, sweaty	When I think I'm going to be late for something important

Figure A1.6 Diary of emotions

Exercise 4.2 (Chapter 4): What you've done to avoid feeling bad

Emotion	Things I've given up because of it	What I miss out on because of doing that
Anxiety	Going out to crowded shops	Contacts with friends, shopping then coffee on Saturdays

Figure A1.7 Ways that avoiding unwanted feelings narrows your life

Exercise 4.2, part 2

Emotion	Things I do to make myself feel better	Effects – short-term	Effects – long-term
Sadness	Eat and drink more	Feel comforted and distracted by food and drink	Feel bad about my eating, weight gain, sometimes nauseous

Figure A1.8 Ways of making yourself feel better and their effects

Exercise 4.3 (Chapter 4): Letting uncomfortable feelings be present

Day/time	Emotion experiences	Physical sensations
Tuesday 10 a.m.	Anxiety	Butterflies in stomach, tension in throat, tingling in fingers

Figure A1.9 Record of emotions and their physical sensations

Exercise 5.3 (Chapter 5): Mindfulness of everyday activity

Day/time	Activity	What I noticed
Tuesday 8.15 a.m.	(Activity 1) showering	Sensation of water on skin, difference in temperature, condensation on shower cubicle
	(Activity 1)	
	(Activity 1)	
	(Activity 1)	
	(Activity 1)	
	(Activity 1)	
	(Activity 1)	
	(Activity 1)	
	(Activity 2)	
	(Activity 3)	
	(Activity 4)	
	(Activity 5)	
	(Activity 6)	

Day/time	Activity	What I noticed
	(Activity 7)	
	(Activity 8)	

Figure A1.10 Record of experiences during mindfulness of everyday activity

Exercise 6.1 (Chapter 6): Old Self/new Self

THEN, I was ...	NOW, I am ...

Figure A1.11 Aspects of Self in the past and in the present

Exercise 7.1 (Chapter 7): Aims in life

Age/stage of life	My aims then
Earliest aims	
Entering adulthood (e.g. 16–21)	
Prior to LTC	
Now	

Figure A1.12 Your aims at various stages of life

Exercise 7.2 (Chapter 7): Identifying your Values

My Values

Figure A1.13 List of Values

Exercises 8.1 and 8.2 (Chapter 8): Values and committing to action

Value	How served in last week	Action within 48 hours	Action within one month	Action within year

Figure A1.14 Values and action plan

Appendix 2

Mindfulness in Western healthcare – background information

Within Western secular healthcare, the term 'mindfulness' started being used mainly following the work of Jon Kabat-Zinn from the 1970s onwards.[85] He established a course helping people with serious medical conditions to cope with the stresses of life, though it was soon being opened up to people with non-medical problems too. Termed Mindfulness Based Stress Reduction (often shortened to MBSR), it taught people certain forms of meditation technique in order to learn to become more mindful, which he described as 'paying attention in a particular way; on purpose, in the present moment, and non-judgementally'. 'Non-judgementally' here means just noticing what is present (thoughts, sensations, breath, or any number of things), rather than getting into judging whether they are good or bad, right or wrong. This approach has spread to many countries across the world, and hundreds of thousands of people have attended mindfulness classes over the last three decades.

Mindfulness Based Cognitive Therapy (MBCT) is a variation that – whilst largely following the MBSR approach – puts more emphasis on dealing with troubling thoughts. It was originally developed to help with recurrent depression,[86] and has since been applied in other settings, including those for people with physical health problems such as cancer.[87]

Within both of these approaches, the term 'mindfulness' not only refers to the mind being in the present moment, but also includes the concepts of recognising thoughts as thoughts rather than realities, and acceptance of whatever your experience is right now, even unpleasant emotions or physical sensations. These are very similar to the concepts of 'defusion' that we discussed in Chapter 3, 'acceptance' in Chapter 4 and 'the Observing Self' in Chapter 6.

However, Kabat-Zinn's approach wasn't something he'd simply invented; much of it was derived from his own background in Buddhism.[88] To a Buddhist, highly developed mindfulness (the usual translation of the word *sati* in the ancient Pali language) is one of the central practices that leads to a life free of suffering. The idea appears to pre-date even Buddhism, going back to early Hindu teachings up to three and a half thousand years ago. To those – like myself – whose exposure to the concept of mindfulness comes through the Western science and healthcare-based versions, the original Buddhist conception of mindfulness includes an emphasis on reflection and considering ideas that seems different from the elements we use in the West. If you want to know more about how Buddhist approaches to mindfulness are being enacted in modern times, the writings of the Vietnamese Buddhist monk Thich Nhat Hanh are well worth looking at.[89]

Like some other practitioners I have met, I was already involved in and using MBCT in my work before I came across the main approach I'm describing in this book (ACT), and many elements of that newer approach fitted very well with MBCT. Interestingly, ACT has very different roots to the Buddhist-inspired MBSR of Kabat-Zinn, but (whether we choose to use the word 'mindfulness' or – as in many ACT texts – 'present moment awareness'), it arrives at a very similar destination: that being in fuller contact with what is actually happening around us and within us in this present moment is incredibly valuable.

Further reading

This book hasn't aimed to be an academic textbook, though I have tried to give a reasonable number of references to key ideas in case any reader wants to check out the evidence for what I've stated.

If you are interested in reading a little further into the topics I've discussed, here are some sources – most of which are already referred to in the text – which might prove useful.

Acceptance and Commitment Therapy

My favourite 'self-help' books on ACT are:

Hayes, S. and Smith, S. (2005) *Get Out of Your Mind and Into Your Life: The New Acceptance and Commitment Therapy*, Oakland, CA: New Harbinger Publications.

and:

Harris, R. (2008) *The Happiness Trap*, London: Robinson.

There's also a very good website linked to this text:

www.thehappinesstrap.com

If you want to learn more about it from the therapist's angle, I'd suggest starting with:

Harris, R. (2009) *ACT Made Simple: An Easy-to-Read Primer on Acceptance and Commitment Therapy*, Oakland, CA: New Harbinger Publications.

then moving on to:

Hayes, S. C., Strosahl, K. and Wilson, K. G. (2011) *Acceptance and Commitment Therapy: The Process and Practice of Mindful Change*, 2nd edn, New York: Guilford Press.

A great deal of useful information about this approach is available on the website of the Association for Contextual Behavioral Science:

www.contextualpsychology.com

Mindfulness

As I discussed in Chapter 5, there is a tradition of mindfulness-based approaches that overlaps with ACT, but is distinct in some ways.

An excellent self-help book based on this tradition is:

Williams, J. M. G., Segal, Z. V., Teasdale, J. D. and Kabat-Zinn, J. (2007) *The Mindful Way through Depression*, London: Guilford Press.

This is applicable to a much wider range of problems than the title suggests. It includes a CD of mindfulness practices led by Jon Kabat-Zinn.

The original account of how mindfulness came to enter Western medicine is:

Kabat-Zinn, J. (1991) *Full Catastrophe Living: How to Cope with Stress, Pain and Illness Using Mindfulness Meditation*, London: Piatkus Press.

If you're interested in the extensive research that's going on into mindfulness-based approaches, a very useful summary of the latest is kept at the Mindfulness Research Guide:

www.mindfulexperience.org

Long-term conditions

For broader reading on individual LTCs, you're really best guided by your healthcare team.

I should acknowledge, though, the following websites used for fact-checking while writing the character studies:

www.nhs.uk/conditions/rheumatoid-arthritis
www.mssociety.org.uk
www.theibsnetwork.org

I found them very helpful, though obviously I'm not qualified to endorse any advice they offer on management of your condition.

Other reading

Although it doesn't talk in the same terms as ACT, I'd recommend for interesting reading on more general psychology about minds, thinking and making choices (including deferred gratification):

Kahneman, D. (2011) *Thinking, Fast and Slow*, London: Penguin.

And in talking about the importance of a sense of purpose, I quoted Victor Frankl. If you haven't read it, can I suggest one of the great works of the twentieth century:

Frankl, V. (1959) *Man's Search for Meaning*, New York: Beacon.

References

1   www.kingsfund.org.uk/topics/longterm_conditions/ (accessed 25 October 2011).
2   Department of Health (2010) *Improving the Health and Well-being of People with Long Term Conditions*, Leeds: Department of Health.
3   WHO (2002) *Innovative Care for Chronic Conditions: Building Blocks for Action*, Geneva: World Health Organization.
4   Mikkelsen, R. L., Middelboe, T., Pisinger, C. and Stage, K. B. (2004) 'Anxiety and depression in patients with chronic obstructive pulmonary disease (COPD): a review', *Nordic Journal of Psychiatry*, 58, 65–70.
5   Sheldon, B. (2011) *Cognitive-Behavioural Therapy; Research and Practice in Health and Social Care*, 2nd edn, Hove: Routledge.
6   Morley, S., Eccleston, C. and Williams, A. (1999) 'A systematic review and meta-analysis of randomised controlled trials of cognitive behaviour therapy and behaviour therapy for chronic pain in adults, excluding headache', *Pain*, 80, 1–13.
7   Martinez-Devesa, P., Waddell, A., Perera, R. and Theodoulou, M. (2007) 'Cognitive behavioural therapy for tinnitus', *Cochrane Database of Systematic Reviews*, issue 1.
8   Howard, C., Dupont, S., Haselden, B., Lynch, J. and Wills, P. (2010) 'The effectiveness of a group cognitive-behavioural breathlessness intervention on health status, mood and hospital admissions in elderly patients with chronic obstructive pulmonary disease', *Psychological Health Medicine*, 15, 371–385.
9   Dryden, W. (2006) *Getting Started with REBT: A Concise Guide for Clients*, Hove: Routledge.

10 Linehan, M. M. and Dimeff, L. (2001) 'Dialectical Behavior Therapy in a nutshell', *The California Psychologist*, 34, 10–13. Available from www.dbtselfhelp.com/DBTinaNutshell.pdf.

11 Butler, A. C. and Beck, A. T. (1995) 'Cognitive therapy for depression', *The Clinical Psychologist*, 48(3), 3–5.

12 Hayes, S. C., Strosahl, K. and Wilson, K. G. (2011). *Acceptance and Commitment Therapy: The Process and Practice of Mindful Change*, 2nd edn, New York: Guilford Press.

13 US Department of Health & Human Services, *National Registry of Evidence-Based Programs and Practices*. Available from www.nrepp.samhsa.gov/ViewIntervention.aspx?id=191 (accessed 18 August 2012).

14 Gregg, J. A., Callaghan, G. M., Hayes, S. C. and Glenn-Lawson, J. L. (2007) 'Improving diabetes self-management through acceptance, mindfulness, and values: a randomized controlled trial', *Journal of Consulting and Clinical Psychology*, 75, 336–343.

15 Williams, C. (2003) *Overcoming Anxiety: A Five Areas Approach*, London: Hodder Headline Group.

16 Padesky, C. A. and Mooney, K .A. (1990) 'Clinical tip: presenting the cognitive model to clients', *International Cognitive Therapy Newsletter*, 6, 13–14. Also available at www.padesky.com.

17 Beck, A. T. (1975) *Cognitive Therapy and the Emotional Disorders*, International Universities Press.

18 Watkins, E., Moulds, M. and Mackintosh, B. (2005) 'Comparisons between rumination and worry in a non-clinical population', *Behaviour Research and Therapy*, 12, 1577–1585.

19 Brosschot, J. F., Gerin, W. and Thayer, J. F. (2006) 'The perseverative cognition hypothesis: a review of worry, prolonged stress-related physiological activation, and health', *Journal of Psychosomatic Research*, 60, 113–124.

20 Wegner, D. M., Schneider, D. J., Carter, S. R. and White, T. L. (1987) 'Paradoxical effects of thought suppression', *Journal of Personality and Social Psychology*, 53, 5–13.

21 Lyubomirsky, S. and Nolen-Hoeksema, S. (1995) 'Effects of self-focused rumination on negative thinking and interpersonal problem solving', *Journal of Personality and Social Psychology*, 69, 176–190.

22 Wetzel, R. D. (1976) 'Hopelessness, depression, and suicide intent', *Archives of General Psychiatry*, 33, 1069–1073.

23 Kashdan, T. B., Barrios, V., Forsyth, J. P. and Steger, M. F. (2006) 'Experiential avoidance as a generalized psychological vulnerability: comparisons with coping and emotion regulation strategies', *Behaviour Research and Therapy*, 44, 1301–1320.

24 Aldao, A., Nolen-Hoeksema, S. and Schweizer, S. (2010) 'Emotion-regulation strategies across psychopathology: a meta-analytic review', *Clinical Psychology Review*, 30, 217–237.

25 Shin, L. M., Rauch, S. L. and Pitman, R. K. (2006) 'Amygdala, medial prefrontal cortex, and hippocampal function in PTSD', *Annals of the New York Academy of Sciences*, 1071, 67–79.

26 Yehuda, R. (2002) 'Post-Traumatic Stress Disorder', *New England Journal of Medicine*, 346, 108–114.

27 Tedstone, J. E. and Tarrier, N. (2003) 'Posttraumatic stress disorder following medical illness and treatment', *Clinical Psychology Review*, 23, 409–448.

28 Ehlers, A., Bisson, J., Clark, D. M., Creamer, M., Pilling, S., Richards, D., Schnurr, P. P., Turner, S. and Yule, W. (2010) 'Do all psychological treatments really work the same in posttraumatic stress disorder?', *Clinical Psychology Review*, 30, 269–276. Available from www.ncbi.nlm.nih.gov/pmc/articles/PMC2852651/ (accessed January 2012).

29 Killingsworth, M. A. and Gilbert, D. T. (2010) 'A wandering mind is an unhappy mind', *Science*, 330, 932. Available from http://scholar.harvard.edu/sites/scholar.iq.harvard.edu/files/danielgilbert/files/a-wandering-mind-is-an-unhapy-mind-killingsworthe-ma-science-2010.pdf (accessed March 2012).

30 Hayes, S. C. (1989) 'Nonhumans have not yet shown stimulus equivalence', *Journal of the Experimental Analysis of Behavior*, 51, 385–392.

31 Kellett, J. (1986) 'Acute soft tissue injuries – a review of the literature', *Medicine and Science in Sports and Exercise*, 18, 489–500.

32 National Institute of Health and Clinical Excellence (2009) *Understanding NICE Guidance: Early Management of Persistent Non-specific Low Back Pain*. Available from www.nice.org.uk/nicemedia/live/11887/44346/44346.pdf (accessed 6 February 2012).

33 Polk, K. (2011) *Psychological Flexibility Training (PFT): Flexing Your Mind Along With Your Muscles* [Kindle Edition]. Available from www.amazon.co.uk/Psychological-Flexibility-Training- PFT-ebook/.

34 Hayes, S. C. (1993) 'Rule governance: basic behavioral research and applied implications', *Current Directions in Psychological Science*, 2, 193–197.

35 Flavell, J. H. (1976) 'Metacognitive aspects of problem solving', in L. B. Resnick (ed.) *The Nature of Intelligence*, Hillsdale, NJ: Erlbaum, pp. 231–236.

36 Harris, R. (2009) *ACT Made Simple*, Oakland, CA: New Harbinger, p. 127.

37 Leahy, R. L. (2006) *The Worry Cure: Seven Steps to Stop Worry from Stopping You*, New York: Three Rivers Press.

38 Iglesias, K. (2011) *Writing for Emotional Impact: Advanced Dramatic Techniques to Attract, Engage, and Fascinate the Reader from Beginning to End*, Livermore, CA: WingSpan Press.

39 Taylor, G. J. (2000) 'Recent developments in alexithymia theory and research', *The Canadian Journal of Psychiatry / La Revue Canadienne de Psychiatrie*, 45, 134–142.

40 Ogden, J. (2007) *Health Psychology: A Textbook*, Oxford: OUP, pp. 221–237.

41 Levitt, J. T., Brown, T. A., Orsillo, S. M. and Barlow, D. H. (2004) 'The effects of acceptance versus suppression of emotion on subjective and psychophysiological response to carbon dioxide challenge in patients with panic disorder', *Behavior Therapy*, 35, 747–766.

42 Wenzlaff, E. M. and Wegner, D. M. (2000) 'Thought suppression', *Annual Review of Psychology*, 51, 59–91.

43 Wood, J. V., Perunovic, W. Q. E. and Lee, J. W. (2009) 'Positive self-statements: power for some, peril for others', *Psychological Science*, 20, 860–866.

44 Fledderus, M., Bohlmeijer, E. T., Pieterse, M. E. and Schreurs, K. M. G. (2012) 'Acceptance and commitment therapy as guided self-help for psychological distress and positive mental health: a randomized controlled trial', *Psychological Medicine*, 42, 485–495.

45 American Psychological Association, Division 12, *Acceptance and Commitment Therapy for Chronic Pain*. Available from www.div12.org/PsychologicalTreatments/treatments/chronicpain_act.html (accessed 13 March 2012).

46 Becker, C. B. and Zayfert, C. (2001) 'Integrating DBT-based techniques and concepts to facilitate exposure treatment for PTSD', *Cognitive and Behavioral Practice*, 8, 107–122.

47 Killingsworth, M. A. and Gilbert, D. T. (2010) 'A wandering mind is an unhappy mind', *Science*, 330, 932. Available from http://scholar.harvard.edu/sites/scholar.iq.harvard.edu/files/danielgilbert/files/a-wandering-mind-is-an-unhapy-mind-killingsworthe-ma-science-2010.pdf (accessed March 2012).

48 Nyanaponika Thera (1972) *The Power of Mindfulness*, San Francisco, CA: Unity Press, p. 5.

49 Brown, K. W. and Ryan, R. M. (2003) 'The benefits of being present: mindfulness and its role in psychological well-being', *Journal of Personality and Social Psychology*, 84, 822–848.

50 Kabat-Zinn, J. (1991) *Full Catastrophe Living: Using the Wisdom of your Body and Mind to Face Stress, Pain, and Illness*, New York: Dell.

51 Bly, T., Hammond, M. F., Thomson, R. and Bagdade, P. (2007) 'Exploring the use of mindful eating training in the bariatric population', *Bariatric Times*, December. Available from http:// bariatrictimes.com/2007/12/.

52 Baer, R. A., Fischer, S. and Huss, D.B. (2005) 'Mindfulness and Acceptance in the treatment of disordered eating', *Journal of Rational-Emotive & Cognitive-Behavior Therapy*, 23, 281–300.

53 Hanh, T. N. and Cheung, L. (2010) *Savor: Mindful Eating, Mindful Life*, New York: HarperOne.

54 Sloboda, J. A., Davidson, J. W., Howe, M. J. A. and Moore, D. G. (1996) 'The role of practice in the development of performing musicians', *British Journal of Psychology*, 87, 287–309.

55 Owen, R. I. (2011) *Facing the Storm: Using CBT, Mindfulness and Acceptance to Build Resilience When Your World's Falling Apart*, Hove: Routledge, pp. 149–150.

56 Brymer, M., Jacobs, A., Layne, C., Pynoos, R., Ruzek, J., Steinberg, A., Vernberg, E. and Watson, P. (2006) *Psychological First Aid: Field Operations Guide*, 2nd edn, National Child Traumatic Stress Network and National Center for PTSD. Available from www.nctsn.org/content/psychological-first-aid (accessed 26 April 2012).

57 Bates, P. S., Spencer, J. C., Young, M. E. and Rintala, D. H. (1993) 'Assistive technology and the newly disabled adult: adaptation to wheelchair use', *American Journal of Occupational Therapy*, 47, 1014–1021.

58 Storr, A. (2001) *Freud: A Very Short Introduction*, Oxford: Oxford Paperbacks.

59 Festinger, L. (1957) *A Theory of Cognitive Dissonance*, Stanford, CA: Stanford University Press.

60 Brennan, J. (2001) 'Adjustment to cancer – coping or personal transition?', *Psycho-Oncology*, 10, 1–18.

61 de Botton, A. (2000) *The Consolations of Philosophy*, London: Hamish Hamilton, pp. 73–112.

62 Snyder, M. (1987) *Public Appearances, Private Realities: The Psychology of Self-Monitoring*, New York: W. H. Freeman.

63 Yalom, I. D. (1991) *Love's Executioner and Other Tales of Psychotherapy*, London: Penguin.

64 McHugh, L. and Stewart, I. (2012) *The Self and Perspective Taking: Contributions and Applications from Modern Behavioral Science*, Oakland, CA: New Harbinger.

65 http://en.wikipedia.org/wiki/Houses_of_Parliament_series_ (Monet) (accessed 25 May 2012).

66 Barnes-Holmes, Y., Barnes-Holmes, D. and Cullinan, V. (2001) 'Education', in S. C. Hayes, D. Barnes-Holmes and B. Roche (eds) *Relational Frame Theory: A Post-Skinnerian Account of Human Language and Cognition*, New York: Plenum.

67 Baron-Cohen, S., Tager-Flusberg, H. and Cohen, D. (2000) *Understanding Other Minds: Perspectives from Developmental Cognitive Neuroscience*, 2nd edn, Oxford: Oxford University Press.

68 Neisser, U. (1994) 'Self-narratives: true and false', in U. Neisser and R. Fivush (eds) *The Remembering Self: Construction and Accuracy in the Self-narrative*, New York: Cambridge University Press, pp. 1–18.

69 Boyle, P. A., Barnes, L. L., Buchman, A. S. and Bennett, D. A. (2009) 'Purpose in life is associated with mortality among community-dwelling older persons', *Psychosomatic Medicine*, 71, 574–579.

70 Owen, R. I. (2011) *Facing the Storm: Using CBT, Mindfulness and Acceptance to Build Resilience When Your World's Falling Apart*, Hove: Routledge, pp. 91–92.

71 Harris, R. (2009) *ACT Made Simple*, Oakland, CA: New Harbinger, p. 191.

72 www.storybookdads.org.uk.

73 Frankl, V. (1959) *Man's Search for Meaning*, New York: Beacon.

74 Knowles, E. (2006) 'Buridan's Ass', in *The Oxford Dictionary of Phrase and Fable*. Available from Encyclopedia.com: http://www.encyclopedia.com/doc/1O214-Buridansass.html (accessed 8 July 2012).

75 Doran, G. T. (1981) 'There's a S.M.A.R.T. way to write management's goals and objectives', *Management Review*, 70, 35–36.

76 Baer, J. and Fensterheim, H. (1975) *Don't Say Yes When You Want to Say No*, New York: Dell.

77 Wolpe, J. (1968) 'Psychotherapy by reciprocal inhibition', *Integrative Physiological & Behavioral Science*, 3, 234–240.

78 Eigsti, I., Zayas, V., Mischel, W., Shoda, Y., Ayduk, O., Dadlani, M. B., Davidson, M. C., Aber, J. L. and Casey B. J. (2006) 'Predicting cognitive control from preschool to late adolescence and young adulthood', *Psychological Science*, 17, 478–484.

79 Cuijpers, P., van Straten, A. and Warmerdam, L. (2007) 'Behavioral activation treatments of depression: a meta-analysis', *Clinical Psychology Review*, 27, 318–326.

80 Gollwitzer, P. M. and Sheeran, P. (2006) 'Implementation intentions and goal achievement: a meta-analysis of effects and processes', *Advances in Experimental Social Psychology*, 38, 69–119.

81 Hayes, S. C., Strosahl, K. and Wilson, K. G. (2011) *Acceptance and Commitment Therapy: The Process and Practice of Mindful Change*, 2nd edn, New York: Guilford.

82 Törneke, N. (2010) *Learning RFT: An Introduction to Relational Frame Theory and its Clinical Applications*, Oakland, CA: New Harbinger.

83 Hayes, S. C. (2004) 'Acceptance and Commitment Therapy and the new behavior therapies: mindfulness, acceptance and relationship', in S. C. Hayes, V. M. Follette and M. Linehan (eds) *Mindfulness and Acceptance: Expanding the Cognitive Behavioral Tradition*, New York: Guilford, pp. 1–29.

84 Behr, E. (1997) *Prohibition: Thirteen that Changed America*, London: BBC Books.

85 Kabat-Zinn, J. (1991) *Full Catastrophe Living: Using the Wisdom of your Body and Mind to Face Stress, Pain, and Illness*, New York: Dell.

86 Teasdale, J. D., Segal, Z. V. and Williams, J. M. G. (2000) 'Prevention of relapse/recurrence in major depression by Mindfulness-Based Cognitive Therapy', *Journal of Consulting and Clinical Psychology*, 68, 615–623.

87 Foley, E., Baillie, A., Huxter, M., Price, M. and Sinclair, E. (2010) 'Mindfulness-based cognitive therapy for individuals whose lives have been affected by cancer: a randomized controlled trial', *Journal of Consulting and Clinical Psychology*, 78, 72–79.

88 Kabat-Zinn, J. (2000) 'Indra's net at work: the mainstreaming of Dharma practice in society', in G. Watson and S. Batchelor (eds) *The Psychology of Awakening: Buddhism, Science, and Our Day-to-Day Lives*, Nork Beach, ME: Weiser, pp. 225–249.

89 Hanh, T. N. (1975) *The Miracle of Mindfulness: The Classic Guide to Meditation by the World's Most Revered Master*, Boston, MA: Beacon.

Index